The Unsupervised Woman
Desperate for Female Friendship

The Unsupervised Woman Desperate for Female Friendship

Oh her soul,
Her sick, sick soul.
M' lady doth lack a friend.
--F. Mazzapica

Have you ever met a woman you had an immediate attraction to–as if she were a long-lost friend? Spontaneously, you just knew that the two of you would be girlfriends for life.

Many of life's longest lasting friendships start out with such explosive spontaneity and a power of attraction and magnetism that seems to ignore differences of opinions, religious beliefs, politics, color, culture, or credos. (Of course, it goes without saying, that I am describing a healthy and wholesome relationship.) And no matter how unintentional this friendship began, or how serendipitous it may have been, both women realized that this relationship was for life.

For the vast majority of women, friendships are a literal necessity. Close relationships between women cannot be ignored or neglected—women desperately need female companionship in their lives (Davis 1985). You will see in the next few pages that female-to-female friendships are actually a matter of health and success.

You as a woman may feel this need deep into your soul, so unlike your male counterpart. Thomas Moore terms this relationship a "soul mate."

"A soul mate is someone to whom we feel profoundly connected, as though the communicating and the communing that take place between us were not the product of intentional efforts, but rather divine grace. This kind of relationship is so important to the soul that many have said; there is nothing more precious in life. We may find a soul partner in many different forms of relationships – in friendship, marriage, work, play, and family. It is a rare form of intimacy, but not limited to one person or to one form."

Moore continues to emphasize that your friendship with a soul make cannot be inhibited. No boundaries or distance, no job transfer, argument or disagreement, or even a lack of order or structure in the friendship, or even lack of plans can stop this powerful bond of friendship you share. Women hunger for a good friendship, for a closeness that describes a special sphere of certain emotions, experiences, memories, and an intermingling of personalities.

Female friendships are often described as intimate–more so than male friendships. Women are more given to transparency, more prone to sharing their inner personal lives (Davis 1985). Many female friendships often share trust, confidentiality, spontaneity, mutual assistance, understanding, and happiness together.

Have you ever noticed, while eating at a restaurant, how often a woman will excuse herself to use the restroom and invite her friend to come join her? Or have you seen a woman brushing the hair of her girlfriend? Females enjoy sharing a much closer personal space than men do. Men may find these practices humorous, confusing, or even foreign, but for women, it is a natural phenomenon.

Women enjoy more friends than men do.

Antonucci (1990) used a term "social convoy" to describe the network of close relationships of a person in his or her life. You would have to agree with Antonucci's findings that women seem to have a lot more friends they socialize with at different levels. Of course this finding doesn't speak for every woman, but generally speaking, a female will have friendship circles in all areas, such as her neighbors, coworkers, church groups, jogging partners, coffee groups, volunteer societies, and even childhood friendships that have been purposely continued in spite of distance or changes of life status. Women seem to hang onto their female friends longer than men do.

However, as much as larger convoys are encouraged and enjoyable to the ladies, they can also prove to be a bittersweet experience. With more friends, it makes sense that this would invite more difficulties.

Larger convoys often see more struggles within the social network, such as death, sickness, relocations, divorces, job losses, marital discord, or other connected hardships that can greatly affect a women's mental and physical health. Female friendships have proven to be so close and intimate that they become a critical aspect of a woman's emotional health, morale, confidence, loneliness, psychosomatic symptoms, and even affecting the ability to cope with other stressors in her life (Lowenthal, et al. 1975).

My wife, Leah, for instance has a tremendous need for close girlfriends. Her social convoy is not only huge, but also unique. She has the ability to secure close associations with folks that do not share her intensity for God or her need for Christian values. Leah also has a large convoy of spiritual women who are very close and needful for her. They pray together, go out to eat, window shop, and plan outings and retreats quite regularly. She is also attracted to foreign women. She loves foreign accents, so much so that she unconsciously mimics the accent of the person she's speaking with. This accent mimicking is our family's enjoyment to watch as Leah slowly and unconsciously attempts to sound just like her girlfriends' British, Afrikaans, Asian, Irish, and Nigerian accents. Unaware, she mutilates the English language in conversations with ladies who struggle with English, almost as if Leah is saying, "Don't worry about the language barrier. I am just like you; we will work this out together."

Leah helped create an "international club" that is made up of women from a few foreign nations–most with thick accents. It is so humorous to watch her engage in conversations from one foreign national to the other–changing and interchanging the accents as she goes. Granted this club only goes out to eat together, or chitchats on the phone and may text occasionally. Nevertheless, their bonds are very strong.

However, Leah, as many women do, will also absorb the pain of the other ladies. She shares in their sufferings and challenges. The deaths of her close female friends have proven to be very difficult on her. Because Leah has an extraordinary mercy gift, she finds it nearly impossible to detach healthily from the challenges of her closest confidants. So when they move, are transferred, or get sick, she experiences major separation anxiety. She still mourns the loss of one of her closest friends who passed away July 15, 1993. To her, Terri died just yesterday if you were to bring her up to Leah in conversation.

Your female friendships help you with success.

Your close female friendships can prove to be helpful in your career success, because women, through their nurturing nature, provide support and encouragement. In contrast, a woman without a close female confidant has proven to bring on social and career isolation, psychiatric illness, poor achievement, failure to thrive in career endeavors, and limited job success in general (Sarason, Sarason, & Pierce, 1989). The woman's network of friends has been connected to life satisfaction, a sense of belonging in all of life and career challenges, increased confidence and competence, and a sense of self-worth. Men, however, tend to be less psychologically reliant upon friendships in general. Men seem to do better when "flying solo" and do not appear to rely on friendship in order to achieve success.

What could happen if you don't establish close female friendships?

Sadly, when women don't have the ability to create or develop meaningful relationships with other females, for whatever reason, it can prove to be harmful to her personality, happiness, and wellbeing (Lowenthal 1975). The lack of ability to make close friends also can cause adversity toward others in the form of personal attacks and coldness. Further, Erik Erickson (1968) stated that an inability for females (as well as males) to make close friendships makes them susceptible or vulnerable to cultic figures and groups that are adverse to society at large.

"Some (lonely and friendless)...opt to follow (cult) leaders who offer them protection from harm of an out-group world as well as group identity" (Hoyer, Rybash, & Roodin 1999).

There are actually two very distinct kinds of loneliness that a woman may face in her life: emotional loneliness and social loneliness. Both of these can create a void or emptiness – and sadness for that matter—inside of you.

"To be lacking in friendship altogether is to be cut off, in a deep felt way, from a richly self-defining way of being in the world." (Moore)

An emotional loneliness is the result of a loss or absence of an emotional attachment, much like the loss or absence of a friend. A social loneliness, on the other hand, is the lack of a social tie, group, or network of friends. Some decades after the turn of the century, it was noted that women of those days experienced far less sadness and depression than the more "modern" woman. The formations of quilting groups and book reading clubs among the local women created the necessary bonding that kept them emotionally and socially comfortable.

Neither of these states of loneliness is a replacement for the other. When you are lonely because of the loss of a close friend, you cannot fill this void with a group of social friends. The two experiences are totally different. You cannot fill the emptiness of the lack of a network of friends just by having a relationship with one person in your life. They cannot be substituted for each other. Likewise, the loss of a lover such as your husband cannot replace the emptiness by filling that void with a group of friends. Your husband, in turn, cannot fill the void for the loss or lack of female friendships either. They are not interchangeable.

Your being lonely is not the same as being alone. We all relish the quality times that we spend by ourselves in quiet meditation with a good book, a cup of hot coffee or tea, walking or jogging, maybe a fireplace to ponder, or maybe even watching a good movie. Some of our most quality-filled experiences are when we have escaped the noise and chatter of the world and just plain get away. But just as alone time can renew and refresh us, loneliness can drain us.

Having close friendships does not mean that the time you spend together needs entertainment or an event. Just being in the presence of your closest of friends seems to be more than enough to satisfy all of us. Aloneness is much like that as well. Though it is subjective, being alone for the renewing does not require an activity or hobby in order to fill the time. In fact, the activity may actually take away or deplete you of your intentions of resting a while. Have you ever gone on a vacation and come back home more exhausted than you left? I believe we all have. You filled your vacation time with activities, scheduled tours, and visiting–leaving you tired and spent.

The life expectancy of a woman is longer than that of man. However, women have a higher rate of illness (Helgeson 1994). Women experience more acute sicknesses and stress-related illnesses due to relationship issues than men do. Some of these differences in physical wellbeing are attributed to how women socialize. Helgeson suggests that females are more affected by stressors that involve relationships. Further, women show greater negative mental health than men do when discussing marital conflicts (Kiecolt-Glasser et. al. 1993).

When there are negative experiences in a woman's relationships, especially her closest friends, there is a negative health issue associated. Not surprisingly, women are at their optimal health and even live longer when there is a positive balance in their relationships.

One common stressor that many wives experience happens when her husband or even boyfriend prohibits her from having close female friendships–for whatever reason. When a man attempts to put an end to a female-to-female relationship— either because he is jealous, confused, put out, self-centered, or just plain controlling and manipulative—he is signing an emotional death warrant for his wife. He may not want to tolerate the constant phone calls, visits, luncheons, retreats, etc. that his wife may be involved in with a close friend. He may be insulting, mean, or will just make things impossible for her to enjoy the relationship. He may not realize how vitally important these relationships are to women. He may attempt to compare his lack of need for such a close relationship in his life or to compare men and women as if they are the same –which they are not.

Why it's harder for you to make or keep friends after 30.

Women (and people in general) tend to interact with fewer people as they move toward midlife, but they grow closer to the friends they already had (Alex Williams, *New York Times*, 7/13/2012).

Below are a few reasons women age thirty and over tend to have fewer friends:

1. You may lack that energy for youthful exploring you once had.

Ten thirty seems like bedtime more and more each day. You find that you cannot stay awake through the Jay Leno Show. You are not the young girl who could stay up all night talking anymore.

2. Your schedule, which is packed with responsibilities and commitments with children, husband, and work, inhibits your social convoys.

When kids appear on the scene, schedules are rearranged by the demands of family, marriage, and employment. You may find that you have less time to talk on the phone, update your Facebook timeline, or even answer your emails or texts. Your priorities have changed. Also, your kids will often pick your friends for you as they themselves make friends and unconsciously merge your families together, sometimes by sheer necessity. Your children's friends need a ride to the soccer game; you coordinate sleepovers for your kids, then there are the birthday parties, the movies, and proms, graduations, and drivers' education. Usually these merged relationships do not survive after the need of coordination subsides.

3. You become pickier with the friends you choose or keep.

The drama queens, egomaniacs, and manipulators don't make the cut anymore. Maybe you have concluded that some friendships are a burden to continue, or that the drama involved has proven too exhausting, or you may have outgrown some friends because you have matured and they have not. Maybe some paths you have chosen to take have made some previous friendships foreign to you now.

4. Divorce often separates you from friends and former family members.

THE UNSUPERVISED WOMAN

You may have been close to your in-laws, but because of a divorce you may have gone through, it becomes awkward to continue close relationships you once had with your former mother-in-law, sister-in-law, or friends of your former husband. Sometimes family and friends "pick sides" as to whom they sympathize more with, which, sadly, puts you on the outside looking in with some of your closest confidants. This experience can be confusing and hurtful for you and others that are involved.

Women need and enjoy the closeness of their female friendships, and as we have pointed out, often benefitting better health and success. Women who lack that closeness, or soul tie, to another female will often experience an emptiness and loneliness inside of them that can only be filled by another woman. These intimate friendships come in all forms: neighbor, co-worker, workout partner, childhood friend, a schoolgirl friend, or a family member. Studies encourage you to covet your female friendships, hang on to them, and relish in the transparency and intimacy that only females can enjoy and comprehend. It's a life source! There's a powerful love that is shared between friends that is surpassed by any logic. The Bible says,

"Greater love hath no man than this, that a man lay down his life for his friends." (John 15:13 King James Bible, Cambridge Edition)

12

And that certainly proves to be extraordinarily true for women as well! Find a friend, keep her, and share life's lessons together. Feel that positive soul tie that will empower you to walk through the fires of challenge and adversity together, and celebrate the joys and triumphs too.

You are more connected to the Body than you realize.

Even though you may not have experienced that feeling of a best friend or that connection to a soul mate per se, your identity is really part of a larger conglomeration of others. We are all connected to one another spiritually. In the context of the body of Christ we are all one body, each of us connected as if we were parts, organs, tissue, sinew, bones, joints, heart, ears, and eyes literally. I think we often miss or rather dismiss this reality. We may pass this off as another simile, but it's so much more than that. We Christians are connected in the same way our neurons move from axons to dendrites to receptacles, through the spaces of synapses – from all parts of the body and then to the brain. We are very much the cells in the blood stream together in the Kingdom of God – all aiming toward the heart. We are branches, limbs, blossoms, buds, almonds, and fruit of the family tree of Christ. However, we often minimize this reality to a mere analogy.

We, the members of the Body, all move about in the King-dom of God, rotating, revolving, spinning, and travelling like the planetary systems and constellations–all under God's

13

supervision. We are not alone in the Kingdom of God. Our souls and spirits are all interconnected. And as the bride, we are all trained and focused on our husband to be, the Lord Jesus Christ. Our steps are ordered, and one Spirit has baptized us all into Christ. So we are not alone. This connection is much like soul mates, best of friends, closer than brothers, but knitted and fused together with greater magnetism and force than any human experience.

Look at these verses from the book of 1 Corinthians, chapter 12:

12. For as the body is one, and hath many members, and all the members of that one body, being many, are one body: so also is Christ.

13. For by one Spirit are we all baptized into one body, ... we have been all made to drink into one Spirit.

14. For the body is not one member, but many.

18. But now hath God set the members every one of them in the body, as it has pleased Him.

20. But now are they many members, yet but one body.

24. But God hath tempered the body together, ...

25. That there should be <u>no schism in the body;</u> but that the members should have <u>the same care one for another.</u>

26. <u>And whether one member suffer, all the members suffer with it; or one member be honored, all the members rejoice with it.</u>

27. <u>Now ye are the body of Christ, and members in particular.</u>

Some parts of the body work more efficiently and effectively with each other than other parts do. They have a closer connection or proximity that has more intensity to its mandate. For example, the fingers work in tandem to make a fist, the eyes work together in order to focus, whether near or far away, the toes work with the foot and ankle to make a step, the two arms work together with the shoulders to carry something, legs sync their striding in order to run, and so on. So it is with gifts, positions, and callings in the Spirit. Pastors are drawn to each other because they share a pastor's heart for a local body. Unlike, let's say, foreign missionaries who work better together in order to accomplish an overseas mandate. They have an attraction to each other that is very deep and real.

This is why it's so important for women to stay close to the body of Christ. To "have church alone" at home is a lose-lose scenario. The church is begrudged your function to the body (maybe like an eye) and you are begrudged the unity of the body that will encourage your gifts and support you. After all, what good is an "eye" without a head to put it in and a brain to interpret and respond to what it sees?

"Not forsaking the assembling of ourselves together as the manner of some is, but exhorting one another: and so much more, as ye see the day approaching." (Hebrews 10:25, King James Version)

Elisa's story

I always took good care of my daughter. She has always been a beautiful girl. She was brilliant in school, won beauty pageants, dated good and clean boys, and never seemed to be attracted to the drinking and drugs crowd.

As my daughter grew into a most beautiful young lady, I was so very proud of her. She was always so kind and polite, and seemed to speak her mind in such a respectful way. I just adored her.

However, when my daughter became engaged to a handsome and successful young man, my husband began to see other women. It totally destroyed me. And as my marriage progressively deteriorated, my daughter's married life seemed to soar with such amazing success never seen by any of our family members. My daughter grew wealthier as my finances dwindled down to frightening levels. She and her husband seemed so happy in their enormous house, while me and my husband struggled with our tiny house and our ruined marriage.

I then began to notice that my attitude around my daughter and her husband was grouchy and short. When they asked me what was wrong, I usually displaced my angry behavior to something random. But the fact was, I had become jealous of my daughter's life. She had it all so quickly, and I still struggled with a cheating husband, a makeshift little house, limited income, and I was aging quickly.

She is beautiful and I am old. She is rich and I am in the lower income bracket. Her house is a mansion compared to mine. My furniture is old; her furniture is custom designed.

Christmas and holidays are now a nightmare for me. My daughter buys everyone fabulous presents, and my contribution is gratuitous. I have been so embarrassed as to my limitations to provide presents for my family. It's like my daughter has taken the helm as the family's leading lady. If she ever found out that I felt like this, I would be humiliated.

I don't know who to be mad at. My husband doesn't make much money and he cheats on me! I am mad at myself for getting old. I know that sounds stupid, but it's how I feel right now. Maybe I am mad at my daughter because she has gotten all of the breaks in life and I haven't.

THE UNSUPERVISED WOMAN

I have struggled for everything I have, as little as it is. For my daughter, everything comes so easy. She's like a magnet to joy and successes. I am jealous of her and I hate myself for it.

CHAPTER 2

The Unsupervised Mother Who is Jealous of Her Daughter

THE UNSUPERVISED WOMAN

The Unsupervised Mother Who is Jealous of her Daughter

"It's hard for a daughter to accept that her mother is that selfish and terrible." --**Alison Lohman**

"I blame my mother for nothing and forgive her for everything."
--**Mary J Blige**

In general, most people are not quick to admit that they are jealous or envious of someone. It's too embarrassing for the majority of us to confess.

If a friend or family member were to accuse us of being jealous or envious of someone, we normally are inclined to resent the accusation. I believe we all would agree that most folks are humiliated by the thought that they are jealous or envious of someone else. The very idea that someone has something in their life that we covet so much as to go to extremes to get it, take it, steal it, and even plot against a person in order for them to lose it, is despicable – but real. And how much more detestable it can be when a parent is jealous or envious of their child, specifically, a mother being envious of her daughter.

Most mothers who are jealous of their daughters can be so embarrassed of their jealousy that they are unlikely to admit it to herself or anyone. She may be in denial until someone brings it to her attention. Certainly, being jealous or envious is a humiliating experience, difficult to accept intrinsically.

We often see the jealousy of a mother toward a daughter in animated films, and it's usually the wicked stepmother who is envious of the stepdaughter, like in Cinderella. But what can be most incredible is when the mother is actually jealous of her own biological daughter.

A mother's pride in her daughter can quickly and even unconsciously turn into envy or jealousy. Mothers, by nature, are supposed to want what is best for her daughter. She may be envious of her daughter's achievements, successes, career, youth and beauty, attention, opportunities, education, and even her confidence.

"You desire and do not have, so you murder. You covet and cannot obtain, so you fight and quarrel. You do not have, because you ... ask wrongly, to spend it on your passions." (James 4:2-3, English Standard Version)

Judith Woods wrote, "You expect your mother to be the ultimate supporter, soul mate, confidant, or even best friend. But she wants the career opportunities that opened for her daughter. She may even begin to undermine her daughter at every turn, and vie for the attention from men that look at her."

"For where jealousy and self-ambition exist there will be disorder and every vile practice." (James 3:16, English Standard Version)

Why do some mothers feel a sense of jealousy toward their own daughters?

1. You may feel like you are losing your daughter.

As your daughter grows older she may seem like she is leaving you, or worse, her growing older seems like you are losing her. It is inevitable that your daughter will attain a driver's license and you will most likely, and maybe reluctantly, purchase her a car. And once she has her own mode of transportation, then it seems like the whole world in within her grasp. She no longer needs rides to her friends, to school, to work; your daughter is becoming independent from you.

"The mother-child relationship is paradoxical and, in a sense, tragic. It requires the most intensive love on the mother's side, yet this very love must help the child grow away from the mother and to become fully independent." --Erich Fromm

The quality of the relationship you have with your daughter will remain intact if you raised her in a healthy way. She will continue to seek your companionship, counsel, and maternal love. No matter how independent your daughter becomes, she will never be able to replace the intense mother-daughter bond. Your daughter will always return to you symbiotically, because no matter how many friends she may acquire in life, she only has one biological mom; and that's you. Though you may need to learn how to accept the new communication between the two of you in an adult-to-an-adult relationship, she is still your little girl deep down inside. It is not strange for college-aged daughters to return home for the summer and to climb into bed with mommy and her daddy for the night, just as she did when she was a little girl who needed the comfort, closeness, and safety of her parents. She won't explore so far that she won't need to return into your arms, because she will always be your little girl.

2. *You may look at your daughter's maturing as a sign of your own decline.*

As your daughter grows and develops into an attractive and maybe charismatic young lady, you may see your aging more vividly, especially if she looks a lot like you did at her age. When your daughter and you stare into the same vanity mirror together, you may see in her face and physical features where you once were in your youth. And as your eyes return to your image in the mirror, you may see yourself where you are and what you have become. For some mothers, this can be a rude awakening of how much they have changed through the years. And though your first inclination may be to grieve the loss of your youth, you may consider the comfort of your growing ability to be relevant to your children, especially your daughter.

As your daughter grows, she will continually need the strength and wisdom of her mother. Your growing child does not need another friend in her life; friends are plenteous and available to her. You as her mother fill one of the most important roles in her life. She will continually need to refer to your years of experience, your vast wealth of failures, challenges, successes, and the big decisions you may have made that can save your daughter from making the same mistakes. You need to grow more mature in your outlook in order to be a help to your growing and maturing daughter.

3. You may feel a loss of your identity associated with your daughter's independence from you.

You have always been the consummate "soccer mom" in your daughter's life. You hauled her to school, soccer practice, band and choir rehearsals, helped gather up her backpack and homework, ensured she had lunch money, and even hosted her slumber parties in your home. You were a member of the PTA; you may have even become a Girl Scout leader, invested in cheerleading, dance, piano, and swim classes. Your entire life was wrapped around your daughter's life. Your identity was largely made up in association with your daughter's identity. And once she outgrew the need of your involvement, you may feel like you are out of a job, and even worse, out of a life.

Everything you did each day was worked around your daughter's schedule. And though you may feel a sense of ease and relaxation, there may be a sense of loss of your identity and purpose.

Empty nest can be a brutal experience for parents who lived each day for their children. When once you said, "It's always noisy and messy in the house because of my children." Now you might say, "It's so quiet and clean in the house, because my daughter is gone." Humorously speaking, I realize that the empty nest for many mothers is well received and deserved. However, to the mother who has lost her identity because her daughter has gone off to college, or got her own apartment with roommates, or has gotten married—take heart! There is life after children!

First, you never stop being a mother. Our children will always need us no matter how old they get. Second, if you are feeling a lack of identity, then consider getting a new life! Consider going back to school, writing that book, joining volunteer groups in your local church, traveling with your husband and mending the emotional and romantic gaps that may have been created between you during the hustle and bustle of raising children. Maybe continue working with the Girl Scouts or band boosters. And get ready to become that grandparent you have only heard about, because when that day comes, your daughter will need your parental skills more than ever.

4. You might feel like you're losing a friend or even a sister.

Some mothers grow extremely close to their daughters. Sometimes the closeness between a mother and daughter grows out of shear survival, maybe because of an abusive husband/father. Maybe because the family responsibilities were so massive, that you could only meet these commitments in a closely related bond. Often a mother and daughter become close due to a personal tragedy that they shared, and only by being together do they feel comfort.

"Mothers and daughters stay connected during teenage years. In the middle of your life, you can become very lonely, even though you're connected deeply to other family members ... and friends." --Holly Hunter

However, as your daughter grows older and your family responsibilities lessen, she begins to look over the horizon of her life and starts the separation process. Independence is natural for all of us. You may feel that you have not only lost a daughter, but a friend or sister as well. However, you are not losing your daughter; she is just expanding her horizons. If the two of you are bonded, then once daughter arrives to her life's destination, she will send for you to become a part of it.

5. *You might have more obstacles that render you power-less to compete with your daughter.*

If you sadly find yourself in competition with your daughter's youth and achievements, you may sense an antagonistic spirit that torments your every thought and activity. Adding to your torment in competing with your daughter is the realization that you are powerless to stop your aging, and that you may have lifelong obstacles that your daughter does not have.

"Jealousy is as fierce as the grave ..." (Song of Solomon 8:6, English Standard Version)

Once your daughter becomes independent, she will be free from family responsibilities, but you still are not. You may be married, which requires a significant amount of commitment, but your daughter isn't encumbered with marriage.

Maybe you afforded a better education for your daughter than the one you had (if you had one!) Your parents may not have had the ability to afford a good education for you, or you might have gotten married early (and maybe had children), which kept you from a higher education.

The list of potential obstacles can be endless for you. And you found that these obstacles have rendered you powerless to compete with your daughter's advances in life.

6. You may have problems in your own life.

Mothers often vent or displace their frustrations, life's problems, and anger toward their children. Sadly, a mother may resent her daughter's life because she personally has found her own life most miserable. Some mothers, consciously or otherwise, have attempted to sabotage their daughter's life or progress because of envy or jealousy.

"People bring their whole personality into parenthood. So if a woman is inclined towards being envious generally, she may end up becoming an envious mother." So says Windy Dryden, of the University of London.

Dryden continues to say that envy is one of the ugliest of human emotions, and it's very hard when you as a mother have such a low self-worth that you are constantly putting down and trying to spoil things for your daughter.

7. You may feel pushed out of the limelight.

Mothers who have enjoyed the attention and sensual attraction from men throughout their life are often never ready to relinquish the limelight. Maybe men have historically stared at you as you held hands with your little daughter while shopping or socializing. But now you notice that men are staring at your daughter instead.

It can be a rude awakening for you to realize that you may not be as alluring to men as you once were. It may have been just a way of life for you as you moved through the public eye. Men staring at you and making the double take as you walked by – you enjoyed the attention because it not only validated you but also just made you feel good. Your confidence soared because you were constantly reinforced as to how attractive, classy, sexy, or gorgeous you were. But those days are becoming rare. Now, your beautiful young daughter is capturing the wanting eyes of men of all ages. You may feel that those staring eyes are rightfully yours to relish, but now your daughter is taking them. This new reality may have created a sense of wantonness and jealousy.

"A tranquil heart gives life to the flesh, but envy makes the bones rot."
(Proverbs 14:30, English Standard Version)

If men have considered you attractive and sexy ever since you can remember, you most likely feel a sense of loss, and maybe wish to hang onto that attention longer than you should. Maybe you find yourself dressing into clothing that was designed for women half your age. Maybe you find yourself pushing your presence more forcefully than before. If you are envious of your daughter's beauty, you may find yourself putting her down in public or humiliating her in front of men, thereby drawing the attention back to you.

The Unsupervised Mother Who is Jealous of her Daughter

"Wrath is cruel, anger is overwhelming, but who can stand before jealousy?" (Proverbs 27:4, English Standard Version)

This is not only insulting to your daughter but also embarrassing for you. Mothers should always be their daughter's greatest fans, and never should they find themselves in competition for men's attention.

How to stop being jealous of your daughter

-Remember that it's her life and not yours.

You have raised your daughter with the hopes and dreams of becoming all that she can be. It's now time for you to let her self-actualize the life you have always imagined for her. This is her life, and she can thank you for your tremendous contribution to her future successes.

-Determine if you are struggling with personal issues of your own.

If you are struggling in your marriage, your finances, and/or physical issues that are causing pain and sorrow, these struggles may negatively affect your relationship with your daughter. Try to learn to separate your personal problems from your relationship. It's not fair to your daughter to become a victim of your jealousy when it possibly stems from other issues.

-Accept your age.

Many women put up a tremendous fight against aging. This fight may translate into cosmetic surgeries, refusing to wear clothes that are age appropriate, and insisting that their social life includes people much younger than they are. Once you come to terms with the fact that everyone must age, and that aging can be a tremendous resource for your daughter, you will begin to age gracefully.

-Come to terms with your limitations.

It may be a startling fact to admit – you are not a spring chicken any longer.

Your body is aging, you may be forgetting things more often, your hair won't do what it used to do, your joints might ache, and you may tire more easily. Yes, we are all getting older, and there are limitations that come with age, and not just with our physical appearance. As we age, our IQ lowers, our grasp of increasing technology may escape us, our taste in clothing will seem alien to younger women, and even our music can be rejected by the youthful listener.

And though aging mothers may be confronted with a myriad of limitations, you are an ever-increasing resource of wisdom and experience. You can rightfully proclaim that you "Have been there, and you own the tee shirt." Your limitations may have closed the door on many areas in life that you enjoyed, but new doors are opening to you if you will embrace the changes—like being an example to youth, having the wisdom to direct your daughter out of harm's way, or the ability to share your accumulated wealth with your children. Come to terms with your limitations and you will see the new life that is afforded the beautiful, elegant, and experienced matriarch.

-Enter into a newfound adult-to-adult relationship with your daughter.

Many parents struggle with the realization that their children are no longer children; they are adults. Your daughter can find it quite demeaning when you speak to her as if she's five years old. As your daughter matures into a young lady, she should be afforded the respect due her. You may find that your daughter may be terse with you because of the way you treat or speak to her like as if she is just an ignorant kid. Daughters have been known to digress in their maturity only when they are around their difficult and condescending parents. Inwardly your daughter will resent you and feel so inadequate when you treat them less than they are treated by society.

-Regard your daughter as an inspiration for you to bloom into a new life.

As your daughter begins to blossom into the young lady she was raised to be, consider growing with her. Let your daughter become an inspiration to you to become a better you! Some mothers can feel that sense of being left behind and other mothers can join their daughters into arenas that they dared not enter – until now. As you daughter completes her higher education, maybe it can inspire you to return to school and further your education. You may choose to take informal classes like painting, design, chaplaincy, literature, or becoming a volunteer at church or for hospital visitation. You've never had time to become involved before, but now there's nothing stopping you. Let your daughter's growth become an inspiration instead of a point of envy. Begin to plan a new chapter in your life that will be fulfilling to you.

-Share your struggles.

Find a confidential friend, a counselor, or minister to confess your struggles with jealousy and envy toward your daughter. The Bible speaks about confessing your faults to each other in the body of Christ. Confession relieves us of our burdens and shares them with the willing listener.

-Bring these issues to God and He will guide you.

God wants to be the savior of all of our struggles, not just the salvation of our souls. He wants better things for you that accompany your salvation.

"But beloved, we are convinced of better things concerning you, and things that accompany salvation ..." (Hebrews 6:9, King James Version)

Some quotes about envy that might help you:

"Envy is the art of counting the other fellows blessings instead of your own." --Harold Coffin

"Nothing sharpens sight like envy." --Thomas Fuller

"Envy consists of seeing things never in themselves, but only in their relations. If you desire glory, you may envy Napoleon. But Napoleon envied Caesar, Caesar envied Alexander, and Alexander envied, I dare say, envied Hercules, who never existed." --Bertrand Russell

"Envy eats nothing but its own heart." --German Proverb

"Come mothers and fathers throughout the land, and don't criticize what you can't understand." --Bob Dylan

"Don't be like Cain, who belonged to the evil one ..." (1 John 3:12, New International Version)
"Help me! Help me! My mother is jealous of me!"-- Unknown

"People envy kids. We'd like to be kids our whole lives. Kids get to do what they do. They live on their instincts." -- David Duchovny

"Envy is not normal." --Terri Apter

God is not done with you.

Mothers who find themselves jealous of their daughters carry such a heavy and shameful burden. Moms who obsess with aging can become emotionally damaging to themselves and their daughter in their pursuit of competition and envy. Envy and jealousy are not fruitful spiritual behaviors. The Bible often refers to jealousy and envy as covetousness, something clearly against God's law.

As we mature in age, God has purpose for us. The same God who started with you many years ago is still with you today. He continually says to you that His plans concerning you are good and not evil, and that He has intentions to bless you and prosper you in all that you believe Him for.

As you complete your first God-given assignments, God will trust you with additional mandates for the Kingdom of God to advance.

"Being confident of this that he who began a good work in you will carry it on to completion until the day of Jesus Christ." (Philippians 1:6, New International Version)

So get ready for God to come to you with new responsibilities, a new calling, that will use all of your experiences and gifts to accomplish His will.

Let's all try to remember that God has brand new chapters in our lives - for each of us. There is enough God to reach to Him for a happy and fulfilling life without having to obsess over what is no longer.

The Family Maiden Aunt
By Judy Small

*Gone now are the years of my halcyon twenties
And thirties are looming alarming ahead
And family members have started their sighing
Indulgently at me and shaking their heads.*

*Cause here I am the family aunt
Oh isn't-it-sad, marriage-hopes-are-fading aunt.
The lonely-future-expectation-laden aunt.
I wonder what on earth will become of me now.*

THE UNSUPERVISED WOMAN

My cousins and siblings in wedding bliss settled
Between them ex-spouses and about fifty kids.
And me, I'm still single, without any prospects
A very sure sign that my life is on the skids.

Here I am the family maiden aunt
Oh isn't-it-sad, marriage-hopes-are-fading aunt.
The lonely-future-expectation-laden aunt.
I tell you what, I wouldn't swap it for quids.

Cause who do you think it is who's always got the time to
play
At gathers of the family clan extended?
And who delights in sharing all the magic of their days?
And gets to give them back again at night?
Yes, it's me, the family maiden aunt.

Oh isn't-it-sad, marriage-hopes-are-fading aunt
The lonely-future-expectation-laden aunt
I tell you what, I wouldn't swap it for quids.

Cause who do you think it is that gets to take them to the
zoo?
Or ferry them for the day?
And who delights in doing all the things they love to do?
And still gets to give them back at night?
Yes, it's me, the family maiden aunt.

The Unsupervised Mother Who is Jealous of her Daughter

Oh, isn't-it-sad, marriage-hopes-are-fading aunt.
The lonely-future-expectation-laden aunt.
I tell you what, I wouldn't swap it for quids.

--From the Judy Small Songbook, Orlando Press, Australia 1986

THE UNSUPERVISED WOMAN

CHAPTER 3

The Unsupervised Maiden Aunt

The Unsupervised Maiden Aunt

"Let the maiden with erect soul, walk serenely on her way, accept the hint of each new experience, search in turn all the objects that solicit her eye, that she may learn the power and charm of her new-born being, which is the kindling of a new dawn in the recesses of space." --**Ralph Waldo Emerson**

Many a fortunate child has been gifted with an aunt who was lovely, gracious, happy, and generous; oh yes, and fun!

Did you ever have an auntie who always knew what toys to buy you and seemed to understand you when no one else did? Did she seem to like ice cream as much as you did, loved board games, looked forward to taking you to the park or zoo? I suppose you loved everything about her. When she had sleepovers, maybe you didn't want to leave to go home. Your auntie seemed to be eternally fun and unfettered by life's responsibilities and commitments.

Though she was your auntie, you kind of wished your parents were a lot like her. She didn't have kids, and there was no uncle around either. She was your maiden aunt.

The term maiden aunt is originally a British term that describes a single, mature woman, without children of her own, who dedicated herself to her nieces and nephews. This is the loose definition of the term. However, to label a woman today as a maiden aunt, one would need to recognize that the term has evolved into one having a negative as well as positive connotation.

Why would a woman choose the life of the maiden aunt?

1. You are probably not married solely by choice.

If you find yourself as a maiden aunt, you are probably not married because of your choosing. You have analyzed the pros and cons, you have watched your brothers and sisters get married, you have carefully recognized your friends going in and out of marriages, and you just feel marriage is just not in your future. As you have watched the heartaches, sorrows, break ups, separations, divorces, infidelities, and sicknesses and deaths–it's just not worth it for you.

You may feel that there's just too much responsibility and commitment for you. Maybe you are afraid that you will just end up with a marriage or family that is full of disappointments and challenges. You may not envy the mother's full-time, around-the-clock tending to their children, the endless chores in providing a home for the husband.

2. You may be dedicated to your nieces and nephews.

"Mother and maiden
Was never none but she;
Well may such a lady
Goddess mother be."
--Unknown

Though you do not have children of your own, you find great satisfaction and fulfillment in helping raise your sister or brother's children. You love them as if they were yours. You relish buying them presents, taking them for outings, babysitting them, and decorating your home and office with their school pictures. However, you also like the idea that you are not carrying the full responsibility of the children. You can drop them off after a long day at the zoo, park, movies, or ice cream parlor, and go home to your much-valued quiet and peaceful life.

You love your nieces and nephews so very much that you probably have volunteered to be their godmother, and promised your sister or brother that you will take them in as your very own in case something tragic happens to your siblings.

3. You may be an extremely religious person–totally dedicated to God.

45

THE UNSUPERVISED WOMAN

"I wish that all men were as I am... It is good for the un-married ... to stay single. (1Corinthians 7:7-8, New International Version)

You may have become so dedicated to God that marriage and children will only detour your divine purpose in life. Many women having this deep-felt need become nuns, single missionaries, or a single woman who tend to the labors of a cathedral, a convent, religious school, or rectory. Some women have dedicated themselves so intensely to God so as to become cloistered, taking vows of silence or poverty, eating meager foods, reading the Bible, devoting their lives to prayer throughout the day, and laboring in small gardens to glean vegetables and fruit for meals.

4. You may be dedicated to your career.

You are a maiden, no woman,
You are slender and faultless and rare,
You are child of my father,
How could I leave you?
        -- Hilda Doolittle

Many women are so entrenched in their careers, that marriage and family would make success impossible. Myriad occupations are populated with single women who value career over marriage. This long and exhaustive list of careers can include doctors, research scientists, businesswomen, politicians, those who travel the majority of the year, entertainers, and so on. It's not that these mentioned careers cannot be coupled with marriage–it's just that many career-minded women do not find marriage as valuable as their married peers do.

5. You may be sexually active but refuse to be emotionally involved.

Many women purposely detach from their sexual partners because of simple convenience and the lack of intentions of staying monogamous. Staying emotionally removed from your sexual partner may stem from an absent father syndrome or other past experience reasons. Keeping relationships simple might be the only acceptable comfort zone.

The maiden caught me in the wild,
Where I was dancing merrily;
She put me into her cabinet
And lock'd me up with a golden key.
                              --William Blake

6. You may be a temptress.

Some women find a powerful sense of control in seducing men. Seduction can be a profitable way of life. Women who know how to sensualize or use seductive powers in order to manipulate or have their way find it quite rewarding emotional-

47

ly, and there can be a reasonable sense of safety involved as well. The temptress can be very effective in getting what she wants, whom she wants, when she wants it. Women with this nature are known to be highly rewarded for their sexual favors and their loose and alluring abilities.

"In the lips of a strange woman drop as a honeycomb, and her mouth is smoother than oil." (Proverbs 5:3, King James Version)

These type women often live alone, possibly as prostitutes or high-level call girls, and may be involved with drug addiction and alcohol abuse. They may sport expensive clothing and jewelry and expect to be treated well by the men who use their services.

You can choose to live a holy life as a Christian maiden.

So, as we have seen, there are women who choose to remain unmarried in order to live a life of licentiousness. But for the Christian maiden, you are greatly blessed and highly favored of God.

Through the eyes of Paul the apostle, you have an honorable status—one of chosen singlehood.

"To the unmarried and the widows I say that it is well for them to remain single as I do." (1 Corinthians 7:7-8, Revised Standard Version)

Your availability to the Kingdom of God is much freer than if you were married with children. You may have found a tremendous peace in your spirit to remain unmarried because God has called you to a special walk with Him; and this is a beautiful and blessed lot in life for those who have the gift to remain unmarried.

Jennifer's Story

Growing up I had always been thin. But when I reached the age of fourteen (eighth grade), I began to physically develop very quickly. So quickly that I became overwhelmed with thoughts of being too curvy for my age. I was very self-conscious about the attention I was getting from seemingly everyone. I felt too skinny for the disproportionately sized breasts I had. It was a nightmare for me. But I also went through a transition socially that began a journey down a road I would have never suspected.

I started drawing the attention of older boys, because I appeared older than I really was. I actually started to date a boy that was a senior in high school when I was still in middle school. I began to socialize with older friends who were years ahead of me in school, because that's where I felt more com-

fortable with the way I looked. My voluptuous figure was more acceptable to them than it was for my peers.

I drove around with them, snuck out of my house after curfew, and began to delve into a life that kids my age couldn't and didn't want to get involved with. My classmates were not as developed as me, so they were always at home, obeying rules and studying, as I should have been doing. As I grew a little older, I was able to get into certain dance clubs that served liquor, without being carded. This opened a larger social group for me that was all quite older than I was, but they never knew it. Though I never had a history of drinking, I started experimenting. I would sneak home way too late and crash all day as if I were a twenty-one-year-old college student instead of an eighth grader. It affected me in such a negative way, which distracted me from what I should have been focusing on. I had no focus on school or grades; I wasn't applying for or even thinking about college like all of my friends were doing. When I finally reached high school, my friends were all about getting into the best universities and talking about different majors they were considering, while I was thinking about older guys, getting married, and starting my life right now by getting a job somewhere.

And I did. I dropped out of high school, got married really young, and worked retail jobs for quite some time. I regret the things I did and the people I socialized with. I am now trying to get through basic college courses that I should have completed years ago. I am still trying to catch up on the years that I wasted. Thank God, I love my husband and my life today. But because of my fast-paced physical development, I felt I had to merge into an older girl's lifestyle that I probably didn't have to.

THE UNSUPERVISED WOMAN

CHAPTER 4

The Unsupervised Woman
Who Matured Early

The Unsupervised Woman Who Matured Early

"I coulda been a contender."
--Marlon Brando in On the Water Front

Sadly, her body deceives us all. She's too young to look so mature. Her physique gives the appearance of a woman; but she is only a lass-of-a-girl, maybe fourteen. Fifteen tops, but she could pass for twenty-one on a good- hair day. She even acts, walks, and speaks older than she really is. Is this girl an enigma, or a description of you as a teenager?

Her makeup makes it difficult to see through to her adolescence. It is a curious delusion of well-brushed and placed hair and tightly fitting clothing—not necessarily vulgar—just more grown up than her age demands.

Who is this girl? She is the one who has experienced early physical maturity. Her facial features and matured body gives her the appearance of a female older than she really is. She is not unique by any means. Our middle schools are well populated by them, not to mention the ninth and tenth grade classrooms. But with the seeming blessings and attention of early development often come a barrage of mixed emotions and dangerous behaviors.

How do the self-perceptions of late-maturing and early-maturing girls differ?

You might have been one of those girls who matured much later than your peers did. Your breasts did not enlarge when all of your classmates' did, your period did not happen until much later than the others did, and if that's not enough–you didn't need to shave your legs during your entire time in high school. You may have found this humiliating. If you fell in among this late-maturing group, your self-perceptions most likely were mixed. Some have a very negative or embarrassed self-concept because they are less developed than their classmates are. Maybe you had a self-consciousness that caused a lower opinion of yourself, or you felt less attractive because you were perceived as underendowed.

In contrast, an investigation of early-maturing girls, who were judged as being physically attractive, concluded that these young women had a higher opinion of themselves in general terms (Lerner& Karabenick, 1974). In another study, girls aged nine to eleven associated (early) breast growth with a more positive image and more positive peer relationships. (Brooks, Gunn & Warren 1989).

Early-maturing girls are often vulnerable to a number of social and physical problems throughout their lives:

The Unsupervised Woman Who Matured Early

1. Early maturing girls will often have older male lovers.

All too often, a young girl with a well-endowed body is ignorant as to why older boys are interested in her. She may find it incredible that an older boy finds her attractive. Maybe the young girl's experience and education in male-female relationships are so void of reality that she quickly finds herself in intense sexual situations that are frightening, fast, invasive, and irreversible. Maybe you were one of those naïve girls who found older boys' flirtations and sexual overtures confusing – but amusing. Strange, but curious. Maybe it made you feel special among your friends.

Perhaps you were approached by a nineteen-year-old when you were but a wee fourteen or fifteen. And, as many early-maturing girls do, you lied to him about your age. After all, you didn't want to lose him or have him think less of you. He complimented you on your attractiveness. You blushed. He offered to pick you up after school in his black Mustang convertible. You accepted with a shy giggle. You worked out the logistics with your soccer mom who always picked you up promptly in her van. You told her that your best friend's mom would pick you up and take you to her house to hang out. And, of course, you'd be back before dinnertime.

You were ecstatic. No, you were freaking out. An older boy wanted to take you out! Whom do you tell? Whom can you trust? More importantly, what do you wear? OMG –it's your first date ever. And if your parents found out, you would be grounded forever, or killed. But you can't resist. OMG! He likes you!

The major problem at this point is the polarized goals of each of the two. The girl has visions of innocent flirting, maybe an enchanted kiss – a peck on the lips ever so lightly, or a hug that sends her transcendent. These are not usually the goals of an older boy. Many mature boys are fighting inner, burning drives of sexual desires and high levels of testosterone. A nineteen- to twenty-one year-old has goals that are far more advanced than the early-maturing girl's aspirations. The matured boy is all too willing to oblige the girl with her enchanted fantasies as long as it culminates in his expectations as well. He will be patient for a while, but just a while. I realize that these descriptions aren't universal, and that not all mature boys are predators as I am describing. But I am a father of three daughters, so allow me some license here.

Early-developed girls learn to link early sexual experiences with love (Magnusson, Stattin, and Allen 1985). I find that this love-ethic rationale is an unconscious effort to feel less exploited, used, or dirty should she decide to engage into a sexual event. This ethic usually makes the sexual act emotionally okay—to keep "love" as the central reason for being sexually active. This rationale works only when the male "lover" cooperates. The male lover will usually cooperate once he discovers that "love" is the main rationale for his girlfriend to have sex with him.

In order to receive sexual favors he may, for instance, pressure her by saying: *"Well baby, if you really love me then you will have sex with me. Isn't that what lovers are supposed to do? So if you love me–then prove it!"* The female normally acquiesces (Cassell 1984).

2. Early-maturing girls have lower educational/ occupational goals.

Often early maturing girls have incredible people skills. They have a natural ability to wax eloquent in social settings. They are often people lovers, enjoy gatherings, can speak well, have a very strong presence about them, are friendly, mannered, and usually have a very strong sense of self. Sadly, however, early-maturing girls have learned to rely solely upon their amazing and advanced social skills and ignore their school studies, their educational goals or occupations (Santrock 1996). If they get a bad grade in their class for instance, they often dismiss the failure and say: "It doesn't matter, the teacher loves me!" What is developing here is that the early-maturing girl is inadvertently relying on her social abilities to gain what she wants, and is ignoring her more important academic skills (Stattin, Magnusson 1990).

If you were an early-maturing girl, it's likely your late-maturing girl friends were at home accomplishing the assigned homework, while you were going to parties, spending hours socializing on the phone, gaining acceptance with an older crowd, and being invited into mature circles that seemed to meet all of your needs. You probably got through high school by the skin of your beautifully white teeth, but sadly, the colleges only accepted your late-maturing classmates (who were just beginning to blossom). Many of your early-maturing classmates, like yourself, got married while still in their teens, had children right away, and experienced financial difficulties. The demands of life, responsibilities of a family, and other commitments did not allow you or your husband to complete college or to attain skills that could provide reasonable compensation for an adequate standard of living.

John Santrock states that many early-maturing girls physiologically grow to be shorter and stockier than their late-maturing girlfriends. Many late-maturing girls will admit that their reliance on their social skills to be a shortcut to success was not well thought out, and attempt to return to school later in their life. It is not strange to see ladies in their thirties and forties sitting in classrooms at a local community college along with students that are their children's ages. In these ever-changing seasons of life, many will attempt to recast their earlier life's goals, some with great success, either meeting or exceeding their initial dreams (Rybash 1995).

3. Early-maturing girls request early independence from their parents.

Do you remember ever saying to your parents in a state of distress or anger, *"I can't wait to turn eighteen (or graduate) so I can get out of this house!"* Many of us said this, but didn't mean it. But some really did have the goal of leaving their family, getting their own place, and leading an independent life without the rules and oversight of their parents. Seemingly, these young people are not setting the bar of achievement and excellence very high if their life's focus is to get out of the house. But for many early-maturing girls, this is step is everything.

You may have grown up so early and quickly that you feel you out grew your mom and dad's effectiveness. You may have found their curfews, rules, household chores, family gatherings, and responsibilities and boundaries stifling and resentful. You found bedtime embarrassing, your younger siblings were irritating, and your parent's judgment was ridiculous and old fashioned. You may have been verbally and emotionally abusive to your parents so they would release you. Though your family may have had wonderful and loving plans for you–these plans were not yours.

4. Early-maturing girls often experience depression and other disorders.

Early-maturing girls often experience eating disorders and other psychological issues such as depression. They are more inclined to smoke cigarettes before the legal age, drink alcohol moderately and excessively, and require some type of counseling in their life. Much of their angst stems from lack of achievement in life. They may describe themselves as unhappy or dissatisfied with themselves or life in general. They have a higher rate of divorces, sickness, and reliance upon government assistance.

When you were younger, you may have also found yourself in a social quandary. Early-maturing girls are often too young to talk openly with older friends, because it's difficult to be honest after you lied about your age. And you might have found it awkward to speak with kids your own age because they hadn't experienced the things you had, nor could you rely on their confidentiality. And of course, speaking to mom and dad about your social and academic dilemmas was absolutely out of the question. These scenarios can create an environment of early isolation and depression.

If I had a dollar for every time I have listened to an unsuccessful adult, who experienced early maturation, describe in detail how popular, attractive, athletic, strong, award winning, or hilarious they were in middle and high school – I would be unequivocally rich!

The Unsupervised Woman Who Matured Early

I can hear them now: *"I could talk the teachers into anything – they loved me; my hair was long and curly; I was the prom or homecoming queen; I had to beat the boys off of me; I could have been an Olympic medalist; I should have been a movie star; I played tennis in school – I should have stayed with it; I should write a book about my life ... I think I still got it!"*

However, I can also hear these regretful remarks: *"I should never have quit school; I should never have hung around those older boys and girls; I should never have married him; I should never have picked up that first cigarette; I should have never dated Tom or Michael."* Their theme song sounds very much like Cher's hit song, "If I could Turn Back Time." Sadly, we cannot turn back time, reclaim words we have hurtfully said, travel back into time to change events that have taken us down pathways that have proven to be toxic.

In your later years as an early-maturing girl, you may come to a place in your life where you will review your past to determine whether your life was meaningful and satisfying or full of despair and disappointment. Some older women have been known to look back with resentment, bitterness, or dissatisfaction. Regretfully, these ladies realized that they were unable to build the life that they really wanted for themselves, and even blame others for their despair. Robert Butler (1963) has referred to this old age tendency as a "life review." Erik

Erickson called this life's review as "ego integrity verses despair."

You Can Still Be a Contender!

At the beginning of this chapter, I cited a quoted a line from the movie *On the Waterfront* starring Marlon Brando, in which his character states: *"I coulda been a contender."* This famous movie won eight academy awards including best actor, best picture, and best director. Though the character of Marlon Brando was a dockworker, he was also an up-and-coming professional boxer. But because of his association with the unions and the mob, he was told to throw the fight, thereby allowing his opponent to defeat him. This was very difficult for the character, but he acquiesced in order to remain in the good graces of his friends, the mob, and the union bosses. Because he lost the fight, and due to other extenuating circumstances, he was never able to achieve greatness in boxing. He knew he could have been a contender had he not followed or listened to the others. And though it may be too late for Marlon Brando's character, it's not too late for you! God has big plans for you.

"For I know the plans I have for you says the Lord. They are plans for good and not for disaster, to give you a future and a hope." (Jeremiah 29:11, New Living Translation)

God says that He will return to you what the locust has destroyed; whatever was robbed from you will be returned to you

64

in an accelerated pace. It's never too late to do something special with your life!

"I will restore to you the years that the locust has eaten, the cankerworm, and the caterpillar, and the palmerworm, my great army which I sent among you." (Joel 2:25, King James Version)

Many early-maturing girls have grown up without having met their life's goals and dreams, yet have chosen not to become angry, bitter, or blaming. Rather, they have found profound concern for others instead of themselves. Maybe you could develop new long-range goals that could help others grow. You may have the capacity to mentor teenaged girls who share the same mixed blessing or early maturation as you experienced when you were young. Maybe you can begin counseling others, assisting those who are sick, volunteering at church, and offering your time and treasure.

"The only thing that can save us as a species is seeing how we are not thinking of future generations in the way we live …What's lacking is generativity, a generativity that will promote values in the lives of the next generation. Unfortunately, we set the example of greed, wanting a bigger and better everything, with no thought of what will make it a better world for our great-grandchildren. That's why we go on depleting the earth: we are not thinking about the next generations." (Coleman 1988).

What about the early-maturing girl who is grown up and has already made bad decisions?

1. Live your life by the Scripture:

"Forgetting those things which are behind, and reaching forth unto those things which are before, I press toward the mark for the prize of the high calling of God in Christ Jesus." (Philippians 3:13-14, King James Version)

2. Live for today!

Too many of us live our lives obsessed with regretting the past and constantly looking toward tomorrow to be a better day. The problem with this is that we totally miss living our life for *today*. Today is very underrated and virtually ignored, being replaced by the regrets of yesterday and the worries of tomorrow. We forget that this is the day that the Lord has made, and I will rejoice and be glad in it! Too many women so mourn their past mistakes that they learn, tragically, to prolong their suffering in bitterness, blame, anger, and even hatred. Start to live your life with a new mandate to help others and to give of your time and treasure. Get your mind off yourself and onto others who need to learn from your experiences.

3. Dress for success.

Do not try to regain your youth inappropriately. Too many women attempt to dress in a way that is not age appropriate. It's actually embarrassing to see a mature woman dressing as if she's a teen or in her twenties. It's also embarrassing to see mature woman trying to redo their youth by exposing too much skin, which lacks modesty and good taste. It's a new day for you, and you can dress in a way that reflects an attractive, classy, and fashionable woman of your age.

4. The good old days were not that good.

Many women want to regain their youth or younger days, but seem to forget how stressful it was as a teenager or a post-adolescent girl. Yes, I know that you long for the youthful body you once had as a girl, but do you remember the stresses that led you to where you are today? In reality, you are right now, living in the greatest hour of your life. Your past is just a shadow of where God has led you to this point. There's a reason why God allows us to see prophetically into the future, but denies us the ability to go back into the past and "fix our mistakes." We are a construction of God that is cemented together all of our tragedies, challenges, and successes. We are a conglomeration of our tears and sorrows as well as our rejoicings and laughter. When you enter heaven's gates, you will be known as an over-comer. But if you had the ability to go back into time and "fix" all of your mistakes, then you would deny yourself the ability to say: I am an overcomer of all of my trials, tribulations, abuses, and bereavements.

"But, beloved we are convinced of better things concerning you, and things that accompany salvation ..." (Hebrews 6:9, King James Version)

SECTION 2:
WOMEN AND MEN

do
not
disturb

THE UNSUPERVISED WOMAN

Gee Gee's Story

My first sexual experienced was with my father's best friend. He was thirty-five and I was fifteen. I fell in love with him. He was so beautiful and he made me feel like I was a lovely lady.

I was not an attractive girl growing up. I know that and others in my family made that clear to me. My oldest sister was absolutely beautiful and was obviously my mother's favorite. I was the ugly duckling that did all the chores in the house–yes, that Cinderella Syndrome thing. I really didn't mind doing all the chores, because it got me away from the rest of the family.

When my quite frequently absent father came waltzing into our house with his new best friend, our eyes met and I fell for him right there and then. To make a long story short, we ended up sleeping with each other. I hated the sex, but was so willing to trade out the sex for being with him; it was worth it. He made me do things that I hated, but I knew it pleased him, so I did it.

I know what your readers are going to think when they read my story. They will say that he was a disgusting, filthy pedophile that needed to be castrated. And your readers would be correct in thinking that way. But the story doesn't end there. I had many sexual partners in my life that were young, old, of a different color skin than mine, poor and rich, and some I actually fell in love with and married. I really don't want to count how many men I have slept with because each one has a different story, and each one of these men came into my life when I was most vulnerable.

I suppose if I had to do it all over again (and I really hate to regret anything), I would have fallen in love with Jesus earlier and stayed single and pure until my "knight in shining armor" showed up. However, I am old now, and alone with just Jesus Christ, And I am okay with that.

CHAPTER 5

The Unsupervised Promiscuous Woman

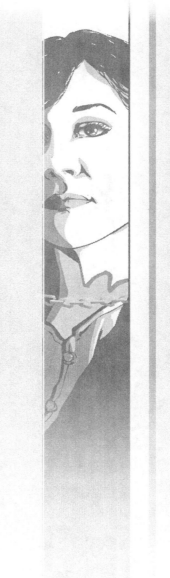

THE UNSUPERVISED WOMAN

The Unsupervised Promiscuous Woman

"I have had sex with forty-two men. I am not sure if this qualifies as me being promiscuous, especially these days. But I guess my concern is that I have slept with enough men that I can't remember all their names; that concerns me." -- Anonymous

The short version of a definition of the word promiscuous would be: Having casual sexual relations frequently with different partners; indiscriminant in the choice of sexual partners. A person who is promiscuous may match the following descriptive: licentious, loose, libertine, unchaste, whore, or a woman lacking sexual standards.

However, if one were to use more slang, colorful, course words to describe a promiscuous women, the terms floozy, easy, harlot, ho, ho-bag, hoe, hoochie, hoochie-mama, hussy, skank, slag, slut, slut-bag, tart, town bicycle, tramp, wench, or whore would be used.

I've heard that women have become too easy. Consider this anonymous testimony:

"My new boyfriend asked me how many men I've slept with. I was afraid to tell him the truth, so I lied and told him only four. So one day I felt that I needed to tell him the truth about how many men I actually slept with. I told him I had been with forty-plus men. I never heard from him again."

How many sexual partners constitute a promiscuous woman?

The question that begs to be answered at this point might be: Based upon the above definition, "Am I a promiscuous woman"? Let's try to answer this question with a few statistics.

In the Hite Report study concerning promiscuous women worldwide, the findings estimated that 45 percent to 50 percent of married, heterosexual women engage in sexual relationships outside of their marriage. The study also found that female Finns have the largest number of sexual partners in the industrial world. British females have the largest number of sexual partners in the western industrialized world.

(In a British response to this study, Britons ascribed to three factors that led their nation as having such a high level of promiscuous women. First, Britain has experienced a decline of religious scruples about extramarital sex. Second, Britain cites the influence of the growth of equal pay and equal rights for women. And last, Britain has a highly sex-valued pop culture.)

Amazingly, the study charted that 41 percent of surveyed women worldwide had been with ten sexual partners, 34 percent had been with twenty partners, 14 percent had been with fifty partners, and 3 percent had been with 100 partners. So, theoretically, if you are a female reader and have had sexual relations with twenty men, statistically you would be in the thirty-fourth percentile of women–worldwide. You may want to use these stats to help you determine whether you are promiscuous or not.

Why would a woman be promiscuous?

1. You may have been raised in an absent-father environment.

The primary reason a woman tends to become promiscuous can be largely attributed to an absent father in her life. An absent father can be a man who is pulled away from his home because of heavy work demands, excessive travelling, divorce or separation, or even emotional removal from his daughter and family. An absent father can also be one who has passed away; he could be physically sick, depressed, have a terminal disease, is a workaholic, have poor parenting skills, or, sadly, has chosen a favorite child over the other siblings.

Daughters naturally cling to their fathers for masculine support, presence, and security. And when that fatherly presence is not there, females will tend to cling to men in order to fill that fatherly void.

Father's play an important role in children's lives. A father can help with his children's self-esteem and build a strong sense of being loved.

"A young woman with an involved and loving father gains the confidence in herself to sever the childhood ties with her father and begin a loving relationship with a man precisely because she has learned to trust men. She has no fear of being vulnerable–a prerequisite for a romantic love–because her father has shown her an example of a man who can be trusted and relied upon. But if she feels betrayed by her father, she will often run to a man more to escape pain than to find love." -- Unknown

Simple things that your dad might have withheld from you like hugs, kisses, tickling, hand holding, carrying, play time, piggyback rides, taking naps together, and father/daughter dates can contribute to a promiscuous lifestyle.

"Indeed, when a daughter is close to her father and respects him as a man and a dad, she begins to judge other men by the same high standards. When she dates men, she will not judge them by their smooth talk but by the depth of their commitment because her own father was not just a talker, but a doer. She will not jump into bed with a man just to please him. She has

78

high self-esteem, and she expects the man in her life to make an effort to please her rather than the reverse. Her idea of a relationship is not going down to the guy's level but raising him up to hers." --Shmuley Boteach, Jerusalem Post

Sadly, females who tend to cling to men to fill that fatherly void often get involved in unhealthy sexual relationships.

"The woman who is too clingy holds onto a man for dear life in fear that he will reject her and leave her like the first man in her life – her dad. The man who she is clinging to perceives her as being too much of a responsibility, so he leaves." Terrica Taylor, The Fatherless Syndrome

Some females may find themselves bouncing from one random relationship to another. Others, fearing the sense of loss and abandonment, will tend to do extreme things in order to hang onto a man in her life. These extreme things can be excessive clinging, suicidal ideations, or manipulative and controlling measures to keep a man with her. Often a promiscuous woman has a difficult time defining love, or has struggled with having an actual love experience. It's regretful to say, but when a woman is promiscuous, she may never really know how to love in a healthy and godly way.

"Growing up without a father maybe the root cause of many social ills – from crime to academic failure." --David Popenoe, Life Without Father

2. You may have been raised in a home where sex was taken too lightly or not seriously.

You may not have been taught proper physical touching, nudity, chastity, virginity, and morality. Perhaps you were raised in an environment where there was too much sexual exposure.

Maybe you had a home life that was filled with sights of random couples having casual sex outside of marriage. Maybe when you were growing up you witnessed your single parents having sexual partners, or your older siblings having casual sex without reprimand. In some households, watching movies and television programs that are filled with sexual content and nudity is more than acceptable. When immortality is not recognized as being wrong early in life, then the possibilities of your sharing the same views is probable.

3. You may have been raised without proper religious scruples.

Many morally liberal families outside of a Bible-based home realize that God has some very strong feelings about sexual activities in and outside of a marriage. The Bible refers to any man or woman who has sex with someone that is not his or her spouse as an adulterer, adulterous, or a fornicator (if neither is married). If you were not raised in a home that taught you about the Bible's teachings on sex, it would be of great profit to research God's position on the subject and the consequences that could follow someone who is sexually immoral.

If you have not established sexual boundaries in your life outside of a marriage bed, you can start today!

4. You may have had a traumatic experience(s) early on with men.

I have recognized that when a woman has been molested or raped early in life, she will often become promiscuous until marriage. Then the woman will not be inclined to have regular sex with her husband. Strangely, though, she may be given to a random or casual act of sex outside of her marriage.

The emotional baggage a woman may carry after a traumatic sexual experience can drag along throughout her life, possible destroying relationships, marriages, and even herself through promiscuous living.

5. You believe the notion that dating must include sex.

It would be beneficial to believe that dating should not be associated with sex, especially when you barely know the man you are dating. If a man genuinely loves you, he will be willing to wait for sex until your honeymoon. If you fear that he will leave you because you refuse to have sex with him, then let him go. If your date attempts to pressure you into sex, then you should make it clear that the date is over and you want to be left alone.

6. You might be trying to compensate for other problems and depression in your life.

Some women may use casual or spontaneous sex with random men in order to drown out the problems in their lives. Sex can truly be used as a drug in order to shield oneself from the pressures of life. In my experience, I have noted that depressed women tend to have more casual sex than non-depressants.

Often, a woman can get so lonely that she may be willing to give sex for love, or sex for companionship. But sex does not usually cure depression, nor should sex be used as the consummate problem solver. Actually random sex can exacerbate emotional problems that are coupled by shame, guilt, and rejection.

7. Are you a sexual predator?

"But I have this against you, that you tolerate that woman Jezebel, who calls herself a prophetess and is teaching and seducing my servants to practice sexual immorality ..." (Revelation 2:20, English Standard Version)

The Jezebel spirit mentioned in the Bible is a spirit that of a loose woman, engaging in immorality, seduction, adultery, fornication, and strives to convince men that it is all right to do such atrocities.

"So many men, so little time." So said Mae West. Are you a woman who enjoys a challenging chase to see if you can seduce a man? And once you have caught your prey, you set your eyes on a new challenge: to prey upon another unsuspecting man, married or single.

I find myself needing to be a bit stern in showing you and all sexual predators that the Bible speaks harshly toward such women.

"But the ... whoremongers ... shall have their part in the lake which burneth with fire and brimstone, which is the second death." (Revelation 21:8, King James Version)

8. Maybe you are afraid of long-term commitment.

The woman who is afraid of or avoids commitment is often quite defensive and guards her heart. She will not allow herself to get too close to a man emotionally. Maybe in other relationships, she fell in love with a man that broke her heart. Now, she'd rather have a plutonic relationship than worry about losing again. It's better to have all the control and not rely on a man for love and a committed relationship.

It's time to give your heart to God.

As we have seen, a woman may become promiscuous for many reasons, but it is not necessary to remain in that lifestyle. Try to realize that you are worth loving. Relinquish your past to God, and learn from mature women of faith how to be in relationship with a man in true love and purity.

"Abstaining from sex before marriage is a wise decision, but it's not enough to keep your heart from being broken. If you give your emotions away to the wrong person – you will still end up with deep heart wounds that God never intended you to suffer. But if you guard your heart and purity, you will be blessed in your relationship. --Whitney Hopler, The Cross Walk

The best counsel I could give if you are struggling with random sexual relationships is to first trust in God and not in man. Tell yourself, *I am better than this, and I deserve better than this. And I know that God has someone special for me.* Second, find a good church, with a good pastoral staff, and a good Christian counselor that can speak life back into you. Once you start receiving healthy Christian relationships, you will find fulfillment in ways you cannot imagine! Last, find a good, organized small group that can support you throughout the week when things get a little tough and challenging.

Christians need more fellowship with the body of Christ than just church services, and small community groups can address your issues on a personal basis in ways that a church service cannot.

A promiscuous woman may find herself having great emptiness, pain, dysfunctional relationships, addictions, and condemnation. You deserve the better life that God intended for you. Pursue a godly future and do not let your past devalue you, because you are truly valued in Heaven by your loving and faithful Father.

Some Long-term Problems that a Promiscuous Woman may Face

-Sexual addiction

A woman who is driven to have casual sex with random partners may actually have a psychiatric condition in her life termed sexual addiction. Let me provide you with a few definitions of a sexual addict, and maybe you may see yourself in these descriptions.

"A sexual addict is associated with compulsive sexual thoughts and acts. Overtime, the sexual addiction intensifies in order to achieve the same satisfaction." --The National Council on Sexual Addiction and Compulsivity

"Sexual addiction is engaging in persistent and escalating patterns of sexual behavior acted out despite increasing negative consequences to self and others. There can be consequences that are associated such as health risks, financial problems, shattered relationships, and even arrests." --The Diagnostic and Statistical Manual of Psychiatric Disorders

Sexual addiction can include: multiple partners, succession of lovers, compulsive fixations on unattainable partners, compulsive masturbation, compulsive sexual activity in a relationship, sexual addiction may also include compulsive phone sex, obscene phone calls, the use of escort services, pornography, voyeurism, illicit exposure or exhibitionism, and even rape.

Sexual addiction is often much like other addiction such as alcohol, drugs, or adrenaline. And other addictions can encourage and/or invite additional addictions as well. So a sexual addict may very well have other addictions such as drugs and alcohol. Many sexual addicts have found help though group counseling specifically designed for female sexual addicts. If you are tired of living an addictive lifestyle, you can get help through a counselor, a support group, a psychiatrist, a minister and church family, and most importantly – God Almighty.

The Unsupervised Promiscuous Woman

-Dangerous health consequences

Whenever a woman is engaged in sexual activity with an unknown person or in multiple random sexual activities, she exposes herself to the possibility of contracting sexual transmitted diseases (STD).

Here are some examples of STDs that promiscuous women are commonly exposed to when randomly having sex with men, especially unprotected sex:

Genital Herpes – Sadly, there is no medicinal cure for this disease/virus. Genital herpes can cause sores on your vaginal or rectal area, buttocks, and thighs. You can contract this disease through sexual intercourse or oral sex. Mothers can also infect their babies during childbirth.

Gonorrhea- can infect the vaginal tract, mouth, or anus. If untreated, it can cause bleeding between menstrual periods, pain and discharge from the vagina, and can also lead to pelvic inflammatory disease.

Chlamydia- infections are caused by bacteria and having sexual contact with someone who is infected. Some possible signs of chlamydia are a burning feeling when urinating, abnormal discharge from your vagina, pneumonia, infertility, and can lead to pelvic inflammatory disease.

When measuring the great danger and harm a promiscuous woman faces physically, medically, emotionally, and spiritually, it should be clear that getting help is essential. An excellent Christian-based support group called Celebrate Recovery might be perfect for you. There is probably one in your area. Local churches usually host them after hours. Try to find a group like this near you – you will be glad you did.

--Unwanted pregnancy

Anger and blame due to an unwanted pregnancy can affect the mother and the baby's health through stress and possible violence. Raising a child in an unaccepting environment is a terrible beginning for any person. A boyfriend or lover who has been distant in the past can become increasingly distant because of the added stress and financial responsibility that comes with rearing a child. Often it leaves the mother alone at home, tending to the baby, while the father works and then finds "busy" things to do to avoid going home. Mom is held prisoner, unable to have a life outside of the unplanned or unwanted baby.

Females usually have three hats to wear: womanhood, motherhood, and wifehood. Two of these are acquired by choice. The other, womanhood, is what she was given by God her Creator. Often, when a woman becomes a mother, she may feel the loss of her womanly beauty because of the demands of being a mother. Indeed, there is often no time for her to pay attention to herself, to feel attractive and wanted as a woman. Everyone in the house needs her, so her womanhood is put on the back burner. This can cause postpartum depression, another serious disorder, if left untreated.

--Post-abortion syndrome

One of the most challenging topics I have to reconcile with as a pastor and counselor is the post-abortion issue. On one hand, I feel the need to provide teachings that include the biblical position on abortion. And on the other hand, I realize that teachings on abortion can compound the guilt women who have voluntarily aborted carry. I totally empathize with women that suffer from the devastating emotional effects of post-abortive syndrome.

Below are percentages of women who suffer from corresponding disorders after having an abortion:

92% - Emotional deadening
86% - Increased anger or rage
82% - Greater feelings of loneliness or isolation
75% - Diminishing of confidence
73% - Sexual dysfunctions
63% - Denial of ever having an abortion
58% - Suffer from insomnia or nightmares
57% - Difficulty maintaining a relationship
56% - Suicidal feelings

53% - Increased or began to use drugs or alcohol
39% - Eating disorders
28% - Attempted suicide

(Statistics compiled from The Elliot Institute)

Living a promiscuous life can invite diseases, unwanted pregnancies, possible abortions, and life–threatening health issues. But there is no sin that God cannot remove from your life—as if the sin was never committed.

Ask God to forgive you, and then by His strength, to help you abandon your promiscuous lifestyle, get baptized in order to proclaim your new life in Christ Jesus, and find a good church to attend. Get to know the pastor, and certainly find a caring support group to join.

Cindy's Story

I was never really a problem to my parents. I never dared cross them. They were very demanding parents of all of my siblings, except for my little brother, whom we all coddled. I volunteered to do the laundry because the Laundromat got me out of the house and away from my parents' demands. I knew that if they looked at me they would think of something for me to do, or I would have to listen to how unhappy they were with us kids.

The Unsupervised Promiscuous Woman

I was not an attractive teen, but one day in school a boy approached me to meet him for a date. He was rough and tough looking, and I knew he had a bad reputation with the teachers. But he was cool looking, and I was flattered that he wanted to go out with me. He was a difficult person; sometimes he wouldn't call me for days on end. And when he did, he was short, to the point, and sometimes cutting and insulting. I really didn't mind it because I was used to this harshness from my mom and dad.

Looking back, I can see that I always seemed to date the kind of boys that my parents and friends could not approve of. I didn't care because I knew that I was most comfortable with boys like that. I guess I was so used to being hurt by my family, it seemed more familiar to date and even marry someone like my father or mom.

I eventually married a man who was older than me, and yes, he was a mean, difficult person as well. I often explained it away by saying that I knew his heart was kinder than his mouth and actions were. He was a thief, a liar, and a womanizer. I knew all of this when I married him, but I thought I was going to be enough to change him into a man that would be decent to my family and me. That never happened.

We divorced eventually and I found myself falling into relationships with men who had all the same characteristics as my ex-husband. They were all inwardly mad and angry people who didn't mix well with the rest of society. The men I seemed most comfortable with were not men I could be proud of. I don't know why I keep falling into this death circle of dating and marriages. Maybe I should marry a better person one day, but I don't think a nice man would want to have anything to do with me. Maybe being single is the best option for my children and me.

CHAPTER 6

The Unsupervised Woman Who Is Attracted to Bad Boys

THE UNSUPERVISED WOMAN

The Unsupervised Woman Who Is Attracted to Bad Boys

"As long as there are men that act like pigs, I suppose there will always be women that love bacon." --**Unknown**

"Being slightly evil could have an upside, and with a prolific love life!" So says Peter Jonason from New Mexico State University in Las Cruces. His study shows that those who score high in personality inventory tests as having criminal traits and evil tendencies tended to have more partners than the nice guys do.

I read an article several years ago in *Women in Spirit*, a Christian magazine, and I thought the following excerpt would be perfect to include in this chapter:

"My addiction was men, and not just any men – the more tattooed, pierced, and party animal, the better. I liked men I knew I could never marry, men you would never leave alone with a child (or a parent, for that matter). The more outrageously different from me they were the better. I was the proverbial good girl attracted to the 'bad boy.'

"Like all addictions, this one started slowly. Not all the guys I dated fit into this bad-boy category, but the older I got and the closer I came to marrying anyone, the further I deviated from my ideal man.

"I was brought up in a fairly Christian home, where my parents were happily married. I was taught to avoid alcohol, cigarettes, excessive piercings, and wild parties. I went to church faithfully and prayed regularly. Yet, I was addicted to men who were completely wrong for me.

"My addiction was so strong that I physically couldn't break it on my own. I reached the point at which I was progressively dating Mr. Wrong, and no matter what I tried, I couldn't be attracted to the good guys anymore. They were too boring, too safe, and strangely too close to what I really wanted, which made them too scary.

"I decided that if I didn't do something drastic with my life, I would be stuck in this rut of Mr. Pierced Tattoo for the rest of my life and end up marrying a drug-dealing alcoholic who blew perpetual smoke rings.

"My idea of something drastic was to move 6,899 miles away to a country where there was limited number of available bad boys. I decided to quit my fairly lucrative, secure job, and serve as a missionary volunteer in South Korea.

"After the shock of arriving in a completely foreign culture, I had plenty of time to analyze myself. This is a scary, life-changing thing to do and extremely important if you're trying to overcome an addiction. I wanted to figure out why I was so attracted to men who were so wrong for me.

"During this time, I prayed a lot. I kept a prayer journal and cried all night to God because of my homesickness, my frustration, and my weakness.

"If you find yourself addicted to men who are not appropriate for you, men you can't comfortably take home to meet your family, men who pull you away from what you really want in life, take a break from dating, analyze yourself, and let Him in. He will lead you to an amazing relationship that will be tangible evidence of God's grace."

* The woman in this story is real, and at the original publication of the article, she and her good boy husband were expecting their first child. (Joanne Truner, "Why Good Girls Choose Bad Boys" *Women* *of* *Spirit* archives www.womenofspirit.com/?id=110)

Let's define a bad boy--

-They have disregard toward others and their opinions.

-They can be arrogant and cocky.

-They can be mysterious, non-committing, and nonconforming.

-They are often vulgar and perverse.

-They are given to disruption, chaos, rebellion, and deception.

-They are attracted to the "gangsta" persona.

-They can be verbally, emotionally, and physically abusive to women.

-They are often combative and possibly wild.

-They possibly appear to have sexy ruggedness to women.

-They are often troublemakers, full of turmoil, mischief, and bad behavior.

-They do not conform to rules and laws, but love thrills, excitement, and danger.

-Many appreciate tattoos, body piercings, motorcycles, or fast and loud cars.

-Their dress code is usually sloppy or shocking.

-They often do not treat women with respect or dignity.

-They are non-sociable.

Why are good women attracted to bad boys?

1. Maybe you are driven to save or change the wayward man.

To you, maybe your bad boy is the greatly misunderstood guy. Many a good woman has suggested that bad boys have a softer side to them, and he will only reveal it to her and a select few. If you have a habit of dating or even marrying bad boys, do you believe you can rescue him from himself? I have heard it said while counseling women with this fixation on bad boys that "there is a sweet, little, broken boy deep inside of him."

You might have said to others that there is a "really nice guy" down deep inside of him just waiting to be released and set free. And you believe that you are the very woman who can do this. And you are willing to sacrifice your entire life, your family, and your children to rescuing this rebel—no matter how much damage he will and has done to you and others. You may have lost good friends because they cannot stand being in the same room with these bad boys you bring home to them. But you persist in this campaign of emancipating the bad boys in your life – no matter the cost. Your bad boy is greatly misunderstood, and if your family and friends could only see the man you see – they would love him as well. Does that sound familiar to you?

2. Maybe you had trouble with a demanding, distant, or absent father.

Did you have a father who was difficult with you? Was your dad a demanding, authoritative man who showed you very little love? I am not suggesting that he didn't love you; I am suggesting that you had to look deep inside of him to find that love. And maybe you have become attached to a man who is also difficult, demanding, and even mysterious in his love for you. You have grown accustomed to just "knowing" he loves you rather than actually hearing the words – I love you.

Many girls grow up with a father who is never home physically or emotionally. Maybe your dad travelled a lot, or he worked nights, or came home late and you never saw him. Absent fathers often produce promiscuous daughters who long for that masculine, fatherly affection and love which they never received. Many women are willing to provide sex to their boyfriends in exchange for that closer male presence. Often a woman who did not have a close father-daughter relationship is attracted to men who are emotionally unavailable, aloof, distant, hard to reach, don't fall in love easily, and have commitment problems. I wonder if you have a tendency to attract these kinds of men into your life.

3. Maybe your father was a wild man.

If your father was attracted to chaos in his life then there is a possibility you would be attracted to chaos yourself. Many women with fathers who were wreck less find comfort in men that live life on the edge, or are destructive and dangerous. I personally find it amazing to see mild-mannered women attracted to violent and exploitive men. Some women who had a father with a criminal record are drawn to men that have a gangster-like personality about them. These types of men have little regard for the law or authority, and certainly have no respect for others' opinions over their own. Sad to say, women suffer in their relationships directly due to how their father treated them as a child.

4. Maybe you feel safer with bad boys.

To a good woman, feeling safe is important. She might believe that bad boys are better fighters than good and kind men are. This would suggest to her that she is safer with a bad boy than with a nice guy. Maybe she is of the opinion that bad boys fight a lot and are experienced with bad people, and that as long as she has him by her side, no one will hurt or violate her. Maybe her bad boy has a presence about him that says: "Don't mess with me or my girl or I will hurt you!" That can be quite comforting to a woman who lives with fear of being hurt or violated. She may be able to tolerate his difficult and devious ways as long as she feels safe in her home or in public with him by her side.

5. *Maybe you can't respect a nice man.*

Do you see nice men as boring wimps whom you cannot respect? Are nice guys nothing more than doormats to you, grovelers who take no risks or chances? Or are they unsexy, goodie two shoes? Women who are attracted to rebellious bad boys often find nice guys boring and predictable, lacking in charm and sexual charisma.

Years ago, I counseled a married man who had quite a lot of money and a new baby daughter. One day, just on a whim (it seemed), his wife met a guy who sported a long ponytail, tattoos, and multiple body piercings. She literally climbed onto the back of his Harley Davidson motorcycle and rode off, never to return. I asked my client why he thought she would do something so strange and unexpected.

He told me that she often said she was bored and felt like she was caged into a life going nowhere. She told him that he was boring, and that being married to him was a dead end for her.

He continued to explain that the man she rode off with was a cussing, drinking, pot smoking, crude, unemployed rogue that had no concern for the family he was breaking up or for the child she was leaving behind. She said that the father could raise the baby daughter better than she could. (And, he has.)

My client mentioned that daredevils, criminals, and strong, alpha males—all of which he was not—always titillated her. Even though my client made an excellent living, this rogue had everything his wife wanted. She told my client that she felt he was always judging her and that she could never measure up to his expectations.

My client was confused by her words. He did most of the housework and most of the raising of the child, never muttering a word of judgment at her. She disliked regular routines, going to church, scheduling meals, and being his wife. She wanted a more spontaneous, dynamic life that brought excitement and unpredictability. She wanted to be free of him and just ride down the highway with the new boyfriend she literally had just met—leaving all of her responsibilities and commitments behind. Does this conflicted woman sound like you?

6. Maybe you feel that bad boys are the best you can get.

Perhaps you have been told that you would never amount to anything and end up marrying a loser. Often we make these statements self-fulfilling. Your parents, family, or even your teachers told you that you were destined to be married to a loser just like you are. Girls who grow up being told that they are unattractive, or dumb, or slow witted, too short, too fat, too sloppy, to be successfully married, end up marrying someone who will treat her as badly as her parents and teachers did. Often women with this type of abusive background will find a bad boy who is less judgmental of her and also considers her parents useless. Though he may be an arrogant troublemaker, and possibly as unattractive as she sees herself, a woman who lacks self-esteem will deem this as the best relationship she deserves.

Can a woman be hormonally attracted to bad boys?

Yes, according to Kristina Durante of the University of Texas in San Antonio, there is a direct connection with hormones and ovulation to an attraction to bad boys. "Under hormonal influence of ovulation, women delude themselves into thinking that sexy bad boys will become devoted partners and better dads," Durante said. "When looking at the sexy cad through ovulation goggles, Mr. Wrong looks exactly like Mr. Right." ("Why Women choose Bad Boys: Ovulating women perceive sexy cads, *Science Daily*, May 14, 2012.)

These researchers at the University of Texas state that hormones have been found to influence women into seeking out men of poor character, deviants, and who have a prowling nature.

The Unsupervised Woman Who Is Attracted to Bad Boys

Are you attracted to the self-obsessed, Dark Triad man?

The term Dark Triad is a psychological term that describes three personality groupings: the narcissistic personality, the Machiavellian personality, and the anti-social personality (or the sociopath). Let's first define each of these three personality disorders as it associates with the bad boy.

The *narcissistic* man has a grandiose self-view. He feels that he is entitled to everything even if he hasn't earned it. He has a massive ego and lives life with a total lack of empathy for anyone. He is cocky, arrogant, selfish, self-centered, macho, and dismissive of any opinion that is adverse to his own. He is disagreeable and believes that he is the most intelligent and capable man in the room. And he is often critical of everyone else who appears to be bettering him.

The *Machiavellian* man is a manipulative and exploiting man who sees everything as potential for self-profit. Simply put, he is an opportunist. He carries himself with a cynical disregard to morality, rules, and only has self-interest in mind. He can be quite deceptive when he offers you some sort of empathy, because he is only offering empathy if it is a means of getting his way in the end. He is willing to say or do anything as long as it will profit him in the end. His motto is: "So what's in it for me?"

Anti-social personality describes a man who is exploitive, paranoid, jealous, controlling, and manipulative. He has low standards for himself, enjoys casual sex, prowling, and deviates from normal behavior. He has been known to be dangerous and even evil at times. He entertains wicked and possibly perverse thoughts, and may even act on them. He performs poorly in social setting, appears to want to push an argument to a physical fight, and can be very embarrassing to be with in public, because he has the propensity to say and do anything anywhere at any time.

This describes the Dark Triad of personality disorders. A trained therapist can identify all three disorders in one bad man. Many of these bad boys can only be treated with medications or a literal miracle deliverance from God.

You no doubt recognize by these descriptions that a man diagnosed with Dark Triad is a difficult and dangerous person. And in spite of these characteristics and traits, a woman may be attracted to such a man.

What does the Bible suggest a woman do if she is attracted to such a bad boy?

Sadly, the American public has a fascination with evil. As did Eve, who was fascinated with the forbidden fruit in the Garden of Eden, Sampson who couldn't keep his eyes off of

Delilah, and even a third of the angels in heaven, who were totally fixated with Lucifer in all of his splendor.

Americans seemed to be lured to vampires, werewolves, horror movies, psychopathic movies, zombies, stories about revenge, illicit sex, haunted houses, and movies that glorify being bad. As a pastor of nearly thirty-five years, I have found that the allure or fascination of evil reaches even into the church body. Many a good Christian woman has been convinced by Hollywood that bad boys are the good boys, that revenge is the right pathway, that good means bad, and bad means good.

Consider this: The film character who kills the most adversaries is the hero. The main actor who takes revenge on another human being feeds our lust for justifiable mass murders. Therefore, it makes sense that many of our good and decent Christian ladies find the bad boy a popular choice as a mate, no matter if he is vulgar, arrogant, deceptive, and even perverse.

The Bible is clear on warning us all to stay clear of wicked men who seek to do evil. Men who are driven to hurt, sabotage, insult, or spread violence to others are a danger for Christians. The Scriptures say not to even set your foot on the path of evil men. Scriptures continue to say that some bad boys actually lose sleep over the idea of wanting to do evil to the innocents. These bad men will not go to bed unless they have first caused someone to fall.

"Enter not into the path of the wicked, and go not into the way of evil men.

Avoid it, pass not by it, turn from it, and pass away. For they sleep not, except they have done some mischief; and sleep is taken away, unless they cause someone to fall. For they eat the bread of wickedness, and drink the wine of violence." (Proverbs 4:14-17, King James Version)

"Depart from evil, and do good; and dwell forever more." (Psalm 37:27, King James Version)

"The wicked watcheth the righteous, and seek to slay them." (Psalm 37:32, King James Version)

"I have seen the wicked in great power, and spreading himself like a green bay tree." (Psalm 37:35, King James Version)

"Abstain from appearance of evil." (1 Thessalonians 5:22, King James Version)

So I suppose the questions presented to you here should be: Why would you want to walk down the road of a bad person? Why would you subjugate your family to such darkness? Is being with a man who will sabotage his and your life worth losing your friends and family over?

Take the counsel of the one who testified at the beginning of this chapter to heart. Get away, analyze yourself, pray to God for deliverance, realize that you maybe addicted to men who are not appropriate for you, and wait on God to put you into a relationship that will encourage all of the things in your life that are dear to you rather than pull you away from them.

Lynda's Story

I am a forty-three year old widow, presently living with a young man of twenty-eight years. I would like to tell you that he is twenty-eight going on thirty-eight, but he is not. But I love him just the way he is.

I was married to my high school sweetheart many years before my new boyfriend was born. I loved my husband; he took good care of me and the kids. He was never unfaithful to me; he was always on time with everything he did. He had a process about him that was so consistent and predictable. He always told me, "Lynda, I will always be where I am supposed to be." That statement put a sense of security in me that I hung onto through most of my life.

I never would have thought that I would be attracted to a young man that is so opposite of my husband. He's unpredictable, sloppy, forgetful, and I find that he is never where he is supposed to be! Why do I love it so? I get so much excitement and thrills with him living on the edge like we do. He never is concerned about being late. He has helped me stop and smell the roses. Do you know what I mean?

I know people are talking nonsense about us, but I don't care. And I know he will leave me one day for a younger girl his age, and I don't mind that one bit. I am going to enjoy the life we share as long as I can.

It's true what everyone is saying. I am paying for every-thing. He has no money to spare on the finer things I can give him. My husband left me very well to do. Folks know he's enjoying the fruits of my husband's labor, but it's mine to spend the way I wish. He's cute, fresh, naughty, and has lots of energy. I like that. I have always been a night owl, where my husband always went to sleep by ten. My boyfriend stays up until three, and sleeps in until noon. I like that we are not in such a rush.

Zoe's Story

I finished raising my kids, all six of them. My husband died a few years ago and I feel like if I don't do something for myself, I'm going to follow after him real soon. Fred, my late husband left me with an incredible amount of money, a paid-off house, and a wonderful insurance policy. Don't get me wrong though, I earned every nickel of it.

I couldn't say that my thirty-five years of marriage was easy, because it wasn't. There were several close calls where he or I almost pulled the power switch on the whole marriage. Fortunately, we seemed to weather it through. I do miss him terribly; how can you stop living with someone for so long and not miss it?

But I feel that I have been given a new lease on life with the empty nest and Fred being gone. So I went to a cosmetic surgeon and had a tummy tuck, a breast lift, and some Botox around my eyes and mouth. I also thought I needed some dental repairs, so I let the dentist give me new white teeth.

I created a bucket list of all the things I wanted to do before I died. I wrote down salsa dancing, parachuting, taking a cruise, and date a young stud of a guy. I know it sounds naughty, but that's just how I felt. I deserved to relive my life over and do the things I never got to do before. I never finished college, but I see no point in it anymore. I feel I just missed out on all the fun I shoulda, coulda had, if I didn't get married so early. I was just nineteen.

I replaced a lot of my wardrobe with what my salsa-dancing friends were wearing, plus I wanted to show off my new bod.

I went home one night with one of the dance instructors; he was a young Latino from Spain kind of guy. I woke up that next morning and asked myself, what am I doing here, and what am I doing with myself? I think I was ashamed ...

CHAPTER 7

The Unsupervised Christian Cougar

THE UNSUPERVISED WOMAN

The Unsupervised Christian Cougar

"The best way to learn to be a lady is to see how other ladies do it."
--Mae West

"In the wild, every female cougar has a cub, from which she never strays far. In the city, cougars have high-powered careers and saloon appointments, so sometimes they need a little help to find their cub and nurture the bond." So says Lauren Greenfield of the Institute Artist.

"Fortunately for the rising numbers of older women and younger men seeking May-December romances, there are as many obliging mating grounds as there are years in between the two lovers. On a recent Friday night in Los Angeles, over 300 cougar "bachelorettes" and cub "bachelors" convened at the Beverly Hills Hotel for the First Annual Cougar Convention.

"While their social acceptability has gone from verboten to vogue, the cougar profile has generally remained the same: financially independent women over the age of 40 with a thing for young men. Today's cougars say that early stereotypes often dismiss the benefits to the cub, giving cougars a bad taint.

Instead of predatory, modern cougars are nurturing, agile, and innately experienced. The cougar convention agrees."

If you as a female, Christian reader are identifying with this profile, you might want to read this chapter carefully.

The term "cougar" is a slang term that describes a woman over forty who is seeking an intense, romantic relationship with a younger man. How much younger is relative to the couple, but twelve to fifteen years difference is average. When the man is over a decade her junior, this would comfortably constitute a cougar relationship.

In my research, I discovered that the term "cougar" was first coined by a Canadian dating website and was quickly picked up by television, movies, advertisements, and many online social networks. Many cougar celebrity couples have been making the news, such as: Demi Moore and Ashton Kutcher, Halle Berry and Gabriel Aubrey, Paul Abdul and J.T. Torregiani; Jennifer Aniston and John Mayers; Jennifer Lopez and her present mate are 18 years apart. The TBS television sitcom called "Cougartown" starring Courteney Cox is a show about older women trying to score on younger men in order to revive their sex lives.

How can we forget (I might be telling my age on this) the academy award-winning movie called "The Graduate" starring Dustin Hoffman, who is being chased by a cougar, Mrs.

Robinson. There is a telling line from the movie where Hoffman says to her, "Are you trying to seduce me, Mrs. Robinson?" The audiences all over the country watched in awe as the cougar woman, at least twenty years his senior aggressively pursued her young cub, until she caught her prey.

Today, the situation in "The Graduate" may not be as difficult to imagine seeing that cougar relationships have become trendy now with mature women increasingly going out with men several years their junior (futurescopes.com).

Why would you want to be in a relationship with a man so much younger than you?

1. Maybe young men are sexually more desirable to you than men your own age.

As men age their testosterone begins to lower and in turn so follows his libido. Ironically, as women age their testosterone begins to increase. Of course, it's much more complicated than that, and everyone is physiologically different. However, in general, these aforementioned statements are true. This may be the reason an older woman is attracted to younger men who can give her a more satisfying time in bed than a man her own age.

2. Many mature women are more self-assured.

Maybe when you were a young married girl in your early twenties, you felt a little unsure about life, marriage, and family. But when you came of age, say thirty-five to forty years old, you no longer wondered about a lot of things. You are no longer helpless. In fact, you are possibly quite self-sufficient and financially independent. And it's been a long time since you've looked for that father figure in your mate. You are now more comfortable with yourself and in control of your emotions. You know what you want, you know what you like and don't like, and you have mastered your feelings. You are in charge of your life and not so concerned with age differences.

3. You might be making a public statement with your young partner.

Some mature women are confident with themselves and what they want, and they want everyone to know whom they are with and what they are doing. They do not care about gossip, because they may actually enjoy the shocking attention. Showing off her "new toy" in society and among her friends and family is like a public announcement that she is starting life all over again, but this time, she's "in charge."

4 .Maybe you view the older man as the old-fashioned you,
and the younger man as the modern you.

The young man is well groomed, refreshing, well dressed,
lean-tight-strong, not afraid of manicures, pedicures, or even
waxing his brows, because he's the new and improved metro-
politan man. He pays significantly more for his haircuts than
the seven-dollar barbershop clip. The young man has twenty-
first century technology; he may even wear a backpack or
shoulder bag, designer sunglasses, stonewashed jeans, muscle
shirts, and carry himself in machismo style.

This is a far cry from the middle-aged man who might be
putting on some pounds, greying or balding, a bit meeker than
you remember him. His clothes are not trendy, and he's going
to bed much earlier than you are. He is more careful with his
spending, and is fine with just a quiet evening watching sports
on television.

However, your energy level is skyrocketing, and you are
ready to go out dancing or skating, and maybe have a drink or
two at a couples' bar that plays current music.

5. You may be feeling and looking much younger than other
women your age.

You may have heard it said, "Forty is the new twenty!"
Well, maybe you have really taken care of yourself physically

and believe you can keep up with the young guys. With new health care, medications, and breakthrough sciences of this century, it has certainly helped put the older generation into a better physical shape. Women who lived in the early ninetieth century had a life expectancy of forty-eight years old. Today, the average woman will live to see the age of seventy-six to seventy-eight years old. We have come a long way in cosmetic surgeries as well. Liposuction, facelifts, wrinkle fillers, Botox, antibody fat medications, new diets and eating habits, and a strong attention to intense exercising have contributed to mature western women feeling strong, sleek, and sexy.

6. You as a mature woman maybe attracted to younger men because it feels good to be the dominant partner.

Many mature women have experienced relationships and marriages where they were the secondary partner. You may also have lived an entire lifetime following first the directions and demands of your father, then the directions of your hus-band, as submissively as possible. However, women who have become single, either by divorce or widowhood, often feel a sense of strength in a relationship with a man many years her junior. After all, because of his youth, he could be a bit naïve, maybe willing to learn from her wisdom and education, and follow her perspective rather than his less developed one.

7. Maybe you enjoy what you have to offer your young mate.

Some older women prefer the role of provider to the younger mate. Maybe she is more astute in sexual experiences, more financially independent, has her own home, etc. She can buy what she wants for herself and for her partner as well. Can you relate? Your worldly experiences may help him with career opportunities, showing him how to conduct himself in certain social settings that maybe foreign to him. Maybe being the primary provider of wisdom and wealth is a pleasant change for you.

So what is the down side of a cougar relationship?

A cougar relationship is not a long-term relationship.

A European study showed that there was a higher divorce rate among couples when the woman was older (U.K. Office of National Statistics).

The relationship was likely not founded on a marital covenant, but more on the sexual attraction. Normally, a relationship brought together on a sexual foundation will cave in unless there is something more fulfilling that replaces the initial attraction. When sex is the primary common denominator in a relationship, the shallowness of this premise will wax old after a while.

Your Christian testimony will suffer greatly in a cougar relationship.

Social perceptions will most likely take their toll on you and the young man.

It is true. People will talk, gossip, misunderstand, misrepresent, and even make up stuff about you if they lack further information. In restaurants people will stare, grimace, and even make comments with the intent for you to hear.

And it won't be any better in church either. The talking and staring will cause you bitterness, so much so that you may leave the church and refer to them as hateful hypocrites and busybodies. However, you knew that this would happen when you got together in the first place, didn't you?

I read an article recently that provided an interview with a woman who was dating a man much younger than she was. I thought that the statement below really summed up the public's perception of such an arrangement:

"We have been together for two years and we get negative reactions from the public. I get the bill at a lot of dinner dates and get asked if he's my son (the question is accompanied by bizarre looks)." (Linda Lowen, "What is a Cougar?" *Women's Issues*)

And the slurs, jokes, and insults that may attach to you both can be brutal. Here are a few slurs I have collected that are regularly used in our society when referring to a couple that is made up of an older woman and a younger man.

-Money-for-company
-Sugar momma
-Sugar baby
-Gold digger
-Trophy
-Toy boy, Boy toy
-Cub
-Cougar
-Cradle robber
-Half-your-age-plus-seven (no, no) rule.
-You are possibly too old to have a child.

A young man usually will want a son or a daughter, no matter what he says or denies. A cougar maybe of an age where she can no longer provide a baby for her young man. It is incumbent upon you not to begrudge a young man his right to father and raise a child that who continue his name and legacy. It's a great responsibility and a huge decision for you to make, more so for him than for you. Sadly, many a young man may abdicate his right to have a child because of his possible obsession with an older woman.

The age disparity cannot be ignored in the family system.

There is usually a negative perception about a woman who wants to be with a man so young that he could be closer in age to her children and have more in common with them. There is dysfunction in the family system when a young man is brought into the home and is expected to receive the paternal respect from adult children or teenagers when they see him as a kid.

As a cougar, your obsession with aging may begin to consume you.

Women are typically more stressed and absorbed with fighting back the aging process. And television, movies, magazines, and billboards that depict attractive women do not make it easy in her attempt to keep up with these expectations. Even though an aging woman may realize that these models are airbrushed, nipped and tucked, provided the perfect lighting, and crimped and painted by the best makeup and hair dressing professionals in the nation, they may still idealize the impossible body and appearance for themselves. And as the mature woman begins to lose her grip on the aging process, she may become anxious or even depressed with her self-image. These anxieties and possible depression will certainly take a toll on the mood of the cougar relationship. Paranoia of the young man finding or wanting a younger girl may haunt, as well as cause much pain and sorrow in communication efforts.

You may have to answer to the double standard of your relationship.

Older men with much younger woman have often been referred to as perverts, immoral, or even predators. However, why is it that a woman, who is obviously a cougar when she lures a young man into a relationship, is not judged so harshly? Is this a double standard?

A cougar woman may wear rhinestones, show a lot of cleavage, dress too young for her age, wear zebra or leopard printed dresses, sport a bikini, and show enormous levels of energy and flirtation. And she can make it clear that her intentions are to hunt for a younger man. But if an older man were to show the same intentions, he is not treated in kind.

I have collected some mixed comments on the potential double standard issue:

"As long as there is no dementia with her, then the relationship is alright."

"Good for her, more power to her!"

"As long as he is not deliberately leading her on for profit, it's OK."

"Mind your own business!"

"I hope she has a prenuptial agreement."

"Ugh, that's gross!"

"Why doesn't she find a man her own age?"

"That boy needs a mommy real bad."

"That old man is disgusting; he should be arrested for dating her."

"He must be very rich for that pretty girl to be with that creepy guy."

Is there any direction and counsel from the Word of God?

- Let's insure that we are not delving into immorality or fornication.

Few things are clearer in the Bible than the commandments of God concerning immorality, fornication, and adultery. You can find that God the Father, Jesus Christ, and Paul the apostle all warned us of the consequences of these actions that truly grieve God. It will be good for us all to remain in obedience to His will. Let's all concentrate on cleansing ourselves of all filthiness of our flesh and spirit so we might perfect holiness in the fear of God. Here are just a few scriptures that might help you recognize God's position on sexual immorality:

"Flee from sexual immorality..." (1 Corinthians 6:18, English Standard Version)

"For this is the will of God, your sanctification: that you abstain from sexual immorality; that each one of you know how to control his own body in holiness and honor, not in the passion of lust like the Gentiles who do not know God." (1 Thessalonians 4:3-5, English Standard Version)

Becoming unequally yoked may present many complications

We often read Scriptures concerning the avoidance of being unequally yoked as staying clear from marrying an unbeliever. However, we can also find ourselves unequally yoked in age, personality, wisdom, and callings. If you are attaching yourself to a young man who is not as wise, experienced, or educated as you are, though it may seem endearing at first, it can prove to be more than an annoyance later in the relationship.

"Now I command you brothers, in the Name of the Lord Jesus Christ, that you keep from any brother who is walking in idleness and in accord with the tradition that you received from us." (2 Thessalonians 3:6, New International Version)

Let's not become a stumbling block or an offense to others.

Paul and the apostles were very cautious not to become a stumbling block or an offense to anyone so that they could remain blameless as to causing anyone to fall. You and I should take great care on how we present ourselves to the rest of the church to insure we don't cause them to stumble. By dating or marrying a young man much to your junior, can invite brothers in the Lord to gossip, slander, insult, and bearing false witness possibly against you. There is just so much we can do to avoid others to stumble, because people will always talk. However, when you present yourself in such a manner that will obviously cause a contention – avoid such behavior.

"We put no obstacles in anyone's way, so that no fault maybe found in our ministry..." (2 Corinthians 6:4, New International Version)

Become a proud and holy woman of age who can teach the younger women how to love their husbands.

There is a proud and reputable role for the mature woman in the body of Christ. That role includes, among many things, to be a good example to the younger women in the church and to teach them the skills and wisdom that you have acquired in your years of being in relationships and marriage.

"Likewise, teach the older women to be reverent in the way she should live, not to be slanderers or addicted to much wine, but teach what is good. Then they can train the younger women to love their husbands and children." (Titus 2:3-4, English Standard Version)

We all had dreams that had to take second place in order to enjoy a marriage or to our raise children. Much of our life as a good spouse and parent has been a life of great sacrifice in order to bring joy to everyone. All of us have had to put our personal dreams and agendas on the back burner, maybe never to be seen again, for the good of the family unit. Be it far from us to regret the labor and toil we invested into our marriage and children as it pleased the Lord to do so. Great will be your reward in heaven for the works you have wrought in your family and as an example to your church.

"He will not forget your work and the love you have shown Him as you have helped His people and continue to help them." (Hebrews 6:10, New International Version)

Lorraine's Story

When I was barely in my twenties, I met a man through my work who seemed to be the perfect guy for me. I knew he was married, and I tried to hide my crush on him as best I could.

He was thirty-five years old and married to what he described as a witch.

When we went on our frequent lunches together, he always shared with me all the mean things his wife did to him. He told me that she was cruel to him and that she never took care of any of his clothes and other stuff that most stay-at-home wives take care of. He was always telling me that he wanted to divorce her so bad, but he worried for his two kids.

Well, one day we ended up in a hotel room together having amazing sex. It was then that he told me he was madly in love with me and that he was going to leave his wife and marry me. I was so excited I could scream. He said he needed some time to get things worked out, but if I would be patient, he would marry me. We agreed that the best thing we had to do was to keep things quiet and under wraps. He explained that it would go bad for him in divorce court if he got caught having an affair. So I did what he told me to do.

For a while, it was unbelievable. He came over my apartment all the time. We had crazy sex, watched old movies, and drank lots of great wine. He taught me a lot of things about wine and about life, because he was much older and wiser than I was. But then things started going south.

After three months of seeing each other, I told him that I thought he would have at least filed for divorce. We got into some small fights that ended with great makeup sex, but he was becoming different. All the cool things he said to me stopped and we were eating more and more fast foods than we ever did. I knew something was wrong, but he said that it was all the pressure of work and his awful wife.

After six months, I realized that he wasn't going to leave his wife for me so I broke up with him. I suppose he lied to me about everything, now that I think about it. I was tempted to call his wife and tell her everything he did with me, but I just left it alone. No sense in hurting those kids; they were beautiful kids to be around even though they didn't know who I was.

I'll never date a married man again. They get all the fun, and I do all the waiting and worrying. I don't hate him as much as I did, but I will never do that to myself ever again.

I got into counseling eventually to help me get over my anger. The counselor told me that because of my age at the time, he was actually abusing me emotionally. She told me that I needed to forgive myself because I was naïve and gullible. I felt dirty and duped. He was a perpetrator and I was the victim. That helped me understand what really happened, so I worked on forgiving myself and vowed to her that I would date only available men my age. And hopefully I will find a good Christian man who wants to be married and have kids.

THE UNSUPERVISED WOMAN

CHAPTER 8

The Unsupervised Christian Mistress

THE UNSUPERVISED WOMAN

The Unsupervised Christian Mistress

"It's never cute or cool being the sideline mistress or other woman."
--Unknown

The self-proclaimed "serial mistress" Karen Marley admitted that she has been a mistress for over fifty men in her forty-five years of living. And she says she has no plans on stopping any time soon.

"Their wives should be grateful when it's me their husbands are choosing, because I am the perfect mistress," says Marley. (Daniel Distant, ""Karen Marley, Mistress, Admits 50 Affairs with Married Men" *Christian Post,* June 25, 2012.)

Obviously, Karen Marley is an extreme example. However, as a pastor and counselor, you would be amazed to hear of the many women I have counseled who lead the life of a mistress-in-waiting. It's actually more common than one may believe—inside and outside the walls of a church. And although a mistress, maybe like yourself, initially finds some temporary satisfaction with her arrangements with a married man, you can be sure that her future will be filled with great anxiety, emptiness, and suffering.

So what exactly is a mistress?

A mistress is a woman who has a continuing sexual relationship with a married man (who is not her husband) or from whom she receives material support. There are other secondary and tertiary definitions of mistress, such as a schoolmistress verses a schoolmaster, a head of a household, or a female who is head of a college. But this topic concerns the mistress who shares an intimate life with a married man.

Originally, in old Europe, the term mistress was actually coined "kept woman"-- someone who was maintained in a comfortable or even lavish lifestyle that was available for the master's sexual pleasure. In the seventeenth and eighteenth centuries in Europe, for instance, mistresses often wielded great power and influence. A king may have had numerous mistresses, but have one favorite mistress or "official mistress" as King Louis XV and Madame de Pompadour. One of the most famous of all mistresses was Catherine the Great who became a mistress to dignitaries after she became widowed from her late husband. Mistresses of early centuries were often kept in secret, but not always. In our twenty-first century Western society, mistresses are typically kept in great secret, and are highly frowned upon even outside those with Christian principles. Celebrities such as Tiger Woods and Mel Gibson, who have shared precarious relationships, have been castigated by the public when caught with mistresses.

Some may be of the opinion that a mistress is merely a prostitute. However, there is a technical difference between the two. A mistress keeps herself exclusively reserved to one man much as a wife would. A mistress most often has an emotional and possibly a social connection with the man, unlike a prostitute who is predominately being paid for a sex act.

Why would a woman feel a need to be a mistress to a married man?

1. I can't help that I fell in love with a married man!

The Greeks are more diverse in their definitions of love than westerners are. Greeks have words that describe the different kinds of love they may feel toward each other. For instance, *agape* love describes the godly love that the Lord has for us. *Eros* is the passionate feeling of love that would better describe erotica, sensuality and love making. *Philia* love is a Greek word that better describes the feelings of love one would have toward a friend. Finally, there is *storge* love that defines one that has loving affection as a mother has for a child.

If a woman feels that she loves a married man, then she should be more inclined to better define which kind of love it is. Certainly having a godly love for a married man will fall short of the purity it was meant to have.

You may have an addiction to this married man you got involved with, which you may mistake as pure love. But it will prove to be an empty and unhealthy longing for someone who is married to another woman.

"...because God is love."(1 John 4:8, King James Version)

2. He's going to divorce his wife anyway.

If the married man whom you are dating is inevitably going to divorce his wife, choose not to be a part of it. Do not contribute to their conflict.

Many men tell their mistresses that they are going to divorce – but do not. They may even tell numerous horror stories about their wives but still remain at home.

3. You share a unique and crazy love.

You may have had incredible intimacy with him, but that will get old real fast. You may one day wake up and realize that he no longer sees you as beautiful as the first day he met you. The unique sex that you both have enjoyed will become commonplace for him. Responsibilities and commitments may bring him back into reality that he has a wife, kids, a home, a career, maybe some savings, possibly great relationships with his wife's family – all of which he will not want to lose.

4. You feel he made a mistake by marrying his wife; he should have married you.

You may feel that you understand him better than his wife does. You listen to him, and share his challenges and problems intently. You may even build his self-esteem, unlike his wife, or so he tells you. You cook, clean, iron, and fold laundry better than his wife does. Your support for him is effortless.

"There is a way that seemeth right to a man, but its end is the way of death." (Proverbs 14:12, King James Version)

He has told you that his wife does none of these things well or often. You may even feel that her house, car, and even kids are rightfully yours because the both of you agree that he made a mistake marrying his wife in the first place.

What possible anxieties and sufferings would you as a mistress experience?

1. Most married men do not divorce their wives for a mistress.

Will a married man actually leave his wife for a mistress? On rare occasions, it does happen. Can a husband really love his wife and his mistress simultaneously? When we live by the principal that God is love, it is not possible that he will love you if he is married. He may adore the way you make him feel, but to love you? No, love is reserved and metered out by God alone. You may be convinced that he does not love his wife. However, I will tell you that he loves his family, and most certainly, it's going to get down to the kids–kids–kids. He doesn't want to leave his children who are his legacy, heritage, and his future. I'm not suggesting that husbands do not ever leave their wives for a mistress. But it is rare. After all, he's not your husband, whether or not the two of you are willing to admit it.

2. You may be wasting your life away while waiting for him to see you.

Sadly as a mistress, you must be the tolerant one of the relationship. You must endure last minute cancellations; you may receive two hours with him every other day, and spend long and lonely nights waiting for him to call on you. You may live for those quick phone calls, sporadic texting and sexting. Your life is in a virtual moratorium. While he is off on family outings and vacations, weekends with honey-dos, and running around with his children's extracurricular activities, you are stuck at home waiting for his exhausted leftovers.

Because you must keep your relationship with this married man a secret, there can be no family and friend parties or holidays celebrations alongside of him. You may feel the relationship and even your life is totally unsatisfying or unfulfilling. You probably live with constant postponements, rescheduling, and always filling the role of the second fiddle.

3. Your life is filled with constant secrets and lies.

You have no open social life. You schedule secret rendezvous in out of town motels, you are careful only to use cash, your local meeting place is always at your house or apartment, and there is no sharing with friends, relatives, coworkers, or neighbors. Eating at your favorite local restaurants is out of the question. Public parks and movie theaters are too risky. You are usually driving in separate cars until you get out of town.

4. The love and happiness you experience with him is not real.

Your life is full of secrecy, constant lying, sneaking around, double-checking every step you both make to avoid being caught, and being careful with hotel receipts, phone bills, restaurant stubs, and long absences. This is not real happiness, and is certainly not real love. God is love. In time, your guilt and shame, conviction and conscience will become overwhelming to you. You may regard him one day as your "sin incarnate."

5. You are inwardly ashamed.

Sadly, if the truth be told, you are a major contributor to a home wrecking, a family breaking, or a marriage breaking.

There is an inner guilt, shame, and embarrassment that are coupled with cheating with a married man. You may rationalize the relationship, but it goes against all of your Christian principles and morals. And although you may act defensively toward those who are trying to help you detach from a married man, you know deep down inside that they are right. Those who are concerned for your wellbeing may clearly see what is happening to you and what will be your sure demise. You may feel that you have an ulterior motive of being with him, such as for his money, his fame and power, or a meal ticket.

Other hurtful and negative emotions you may feel as a mistress.

-You may begin to distrust all men as cheaters.

-You may feel that you must hide that you are a mistress forever.

-You may feel revengeful toward him and his family (fatal attraction).

-*You may fear the possibility of pregnancy (or actually become pregnant), which will really complicate things.*

-*Other women who find out you are a mistress will not trust you around their husbands. This can cause much alienation from you.*

-*Mistresses may suffer from low self-esteem and lack of self-respect.*

-*You may lose a lot of precious personal time, a sense of freedom, youth, and beauty while you wait for him to divorce his wife.*

-*If his wife finds out about your affair with her husband, he may blame you for seducing him.*

-*He may distrust you if he thinks you are seeing another man.*

-*You may feel that he has another mistress other than you.*

-*Sadly, with you on the sideline and his wife in his bed each day, you will feel that "he has his cake and is eating it too."*

-*If he actually does marry you, you know he historically doesn't respect the institution of marriage. He may cheat on you too.*

Some hints that he is going to leave you and go back to his wife and family:

-He is distancing himself from you.

-He is looking to cause or prolong a fight with you.

-His cancellations, postponements, and no-shows are becoming more frequent.

-He seems defensive about his wife.

-He stops using your pet name.

-Seems indifferent toward you.

-Doesn't seem as excited to jump into bed with you as he once did. Nor does he seem romantic. He actually pulls away from your affectionate advances. He tells you that sex was extraordinary but now it has become just ordinary between the two of you.

-No more pillow talk. He no longer stares into your eyes or spoons you, but rather stares off in deep thought, or rolls over and falls asleep, or worst yet, he gets out of the bed puts his clothes on, and rushes back to his family.

-He may feel you are becoming less attractive or sexy to him.

-He doesn't ask you about your day.

-He doesn't share conversation about his day.

-He is uncharacteristically crude, rude, short, disrespectful, cold, or impatient. He possibly begins to refer to your relationship with him as a "fling" or a mistake.

-He stops buying you gifts or bringing you some of your favorite fun foods.

He explains that it's becoming too expensive to support two women. He may say that it can be very costly to run two households, and he's going to be more inclined to provide for his family before he provides for you.

-His compliments toward you have all but ceased.

-He takes longer to return your calls or texts, and doesn't participate in sexting or returning your "I love yous" like he used to.

-He's treating you like he treated his wife by saying he's working late, taking business trips, having boys' nights out, or picking a fight with you so he can storm out.

It's time for you to break it off with the married man.

I think you will agree with me that it's time that you say to yourself, *"My life is not for rent anymore."* You are better than that, and you deserve more than he is giving you. We need to fight back the fear, the tears, the potential codependency, and the false hopes that things will be better once he leaves his wife and family. After all, it's been years; why would he change now?

You need to write him a "Dear John" letter or confront him face-to-face and say: "I'm sorry but I can't see you anymore. You and your wife need to see a good marriage counselor and give it another chance. But for me, I am going to get back to respecting myself and give myself a better life."

Here's a sample to get you started.

Dear John:

I am leaving you.

I thought the love I had for you would be enough justification to endure the hardships of waiting for you to be available to me, but I see now that it was not true.

I cannot continue my life as the second fiddle any longer. It's not fair to me. I am going to take my life off hold and begin to enjoy the things I once had before I met you. I

hold no anger toward you; I somehow knew what I was getting into, but I just didn't want to admit it to myself. I can't believe that I was willing to be "the other woman" and to be a part of breaking up someone's marriage, even if it is falling apart. I ask you to forgive me for contributing to your marital hardships. I pray that things work out with your wife and children.

Please don't contact me any further. I need to pull myself together emotionally and spiritually, and I don't need any more complications than I already have.

As for me, I am going to ask God to forgive me for the sins I committed with you, and get back into my local church I love so dearly. I am going to get some counseling to help me get some reasonable health back into my life so I can be of some value to the man God has for me.

Sincerely,

Jane

A mistress should take deliberate steps to end the affair for her own good:

-Immediately break up with the married man.

-Do not contact the married man ever again, and ensure that he does not contact you as well. If he pursues you, tell him if he doesn't stop, you will contact his wife.

-Seek Christian counselors for recovery.

-Find a Celebrate Recovery group (or a Christian support group) in your area for support and a sponsor.

-Confess your faults with certain friends who can help you recover.

-Ask God to forgive you and to give you strength to never fall for that satanic snare ever again.

-Get back to your life!

-Make a wish list of characteristics and traits you want in a man you wish to marry.

-Seek to become the consummate Proverbs 31 woman you were meant to be!

Rachel's Story

I think I keep getting married because I mistake liking someone for loving. And I am realizing now, late in life, that love is just not enough for me. I seem to be attracted to projects; that is, men who need my help to "fix" them.

I like the feeling of being needed, so I want to be involved with a man that I can contribute to his survival. That feeling of being needed to me means that he wants me and loves me. I know that's wrong to think that way, because once he gets better, I am virtually out of a job. So they usually leave me. When I sense that my husband is getting healthier, I get scared so I begin to unconsciously torment him until he needs fixing again; I sabotage the marriage. After all, I don't want him to leave me. It's just a vicious cycle I get myself into. I wish I had enough belief in myself that I could marry a mentally healthy man, but I know I won't feel loved and accepted unless I can contribute to the marriage in my own sick way – and that's by fixing him.

Marrying healthy men frightens me. I have dated men who are healthy, and I don't know what to do. I am an attractive woman so I know that they like what they see, but that won't last forever. Once a man gets tired of sleeping with me, I feel he will leave me because he's so healthy and I'm so needy. I guess I am a high-maintenance woman when I am not fixing my husband.

I see other wives who don't seem to struggle with worrying about how much they contribute to a marriage. I envy that; I wish that I could believe in myself enough to say that he just wants me the way I am. I get it logically, but I have that fear in me that says I am not enough to keep him interested in me. I have been to counselors, and read lots of self-help books, but I'm still afraid to marry men who don't need me to fix them all the time. I date men that have addictions, low self-esteem, and men that have children that need me to mother them. And these men of my past have always gotten angry with me because I drop the ball on helping them. It's probably because I know that it's not fair to me to have to work so hard to keep them from leaving me.

I read stories about the young woman that marries a medical student. She works hard in order to provide financially until he passes his medical boards. And once he becomes a doctor, he divorces the woman that worked so hard for him and replaces her with a trophy wife. That angers me, but that's me in a nutshell.

CHAPTER 9

The Unsupervised Woman
Who Marries a Lot

The Unsupervised Woman Who Marries a Lot

"To the married I give this commandment (not I, but the Lord): a wife must not separate from her husband." --1 Corinthians 7:10, New International Version

Do you know which woman has been married the most times in recorded history?

No, it's not Zsa Zsa Gabor though she's been married nine times. And it's not Elizabeth Taylor with all of her seven ex-husbands. Not Joan Collins with her five, or even Liza Minnelli with her four ex-husbands.

Her name is Linda Wolfe, hailing from the great State of Indiana. She has been married for a whopping 23 times! Linda emphatically believes that the reason why she has been married so many times is because, *"I'm addicted to romance."*

Though she can't remember all of her husbands in order, she can name them and each of their respective employments. She has married a one-eyed convict, a preacher, a musician, a few bartenders, a homeless man, some electricians and plumbers, two gay men, married to the same man three times, one beat her, more than one abandoned her, and she's on the lookout for number twenty-four.

The longest marriage she had was with her first husband. That marriage lasted seven years. Linda's shortest marriage experience lasted only thirty-six hours. When asked why the marriage ended so quickly, she stated: "The love just wasn't there." And with seven children in her quiver, she says she's never cheated on any of her twenty-three husbands.

Linda told the Indianapolis Star: "It's been years since I walked the aisle; I miss it. I would get married again, because you know, it gets lonely."

What's the reason for marrying so much?

Women who have been married many times have been called many things: hopeless romantic, serial bride, repeat bride, honeymoon bride, promiscuous and unstable, a poor judge of character, uncommitted, or just a plain laughing stock.

Why are these marriage addicts willing to go back into one marriage after the next, regardless as to how many times they have walked the aisle, ordered flowers, sent out invitations, arranged for bridesmaids, rented out catering halls, met with the clergy, or unabashed in repeating: "I do" again, again, and again, and again"?

The Unsupervised Woman Who Marries a Lot

But what are these women saying about themselves?

-Being single is a stigma.

-I don't want to be alone.

-I need financial security.

-I want to have children.

-I keep getting pregnant.

-I always ignore all the obvious warning signs!

-I think all good girls should be married.

-I keep thinking that this one is for real!

-I need the security of belonging to someone.

-I believe being married is more acceptable in society.

-I fall in love real easy.

What are the statistics regarding remarriage?

I know statistics can get quite boring, but we can learn from them.

The U.S. Census surveys from a decade ago show that 3 percent of people were married three times or more, compared to the 14 percent that were married twice. Typically, first marriages last for eleven years, and the average age for a first divorce is thirty-seven to forty-two. But, second marriages are nearly twice as likely to fail as first ones, and those having been married three times are three times more likely to be divorced.

According to Top54U, published February 2010:

-One-fifth of first marriages end within five years.
-One-third of marriages will end in ten years.
-75 percent of divorced women will remarry within ten years.

Here's the extraordinary data:

-74 percent of marriages in the USA end in divorce.
-60 percent to 80 percent of remarriages end in divorce (depending on first, second, or third remarriage).

Remarriage can be affected by ethnicity.

The census also shows that divorces and remarriages differ by ethnicity. Remarriage is most common among white women, while black women have the lowest probability to remarry.

Remarriage can be based on age of the woman.

Age is also a factor in determining whether a woman will remarry. For instance, women that are twenty-five and older are less likely to remarry than a woman who is younger than twenty-five.

Remarriage can be affected by certain demographics.

Women of urban areas are less likely to marry again as compared to rural women.

Remarriages can cause death.

Those married three times were a third more likely to die earlier than those who marry once for life. Thirty-four percent of people married three or more times are likely to die just after their fiftieth birthday. The stress of repeated bad marriages can contribute to an early death.

What are some reasons that you consider marrying many times?

You may be jumping into relationships much too quickly. Using bad dating strategies, and not seeking professional counselors, clergy, or the opinions of friends and family.

You may be attracted to the same kind of guy that does not share your personal ideals, but you may feel that he will change after he marries you. A woman may say that her boyfriend is a nice guy, and though she may not be in love with him, she imagines that the marriage will probably work out. If this is your position on the marriage before the ceremony, you might want to reconsider. If he will not change before you marry, he will certainly not change after the ceremony.

Many women need to learn how to rid themselves of old baggage from prior relationships before they involve themselves with another man. Some ladies are just repeating the same mistakes of the last relationship or marriage. And they carry these unresolved issues, intimate or otherwise, right into the next marriage—issues that contributed to the previous divorce. Are you carrying a lot of baggage around with you, lugging the problems from relationship to relationship?

Are you prone to not adapting, compromising, or being willing to deal with the pressures of a relationship? Some women find no value in bothering with the troubles that come into a marriage, so divorce becomes a logical next step for them. They have been married and divorced so many times that the fear of divorcing just isn't a factor. If you find yourself historically inflexible in your relationships, then you should consider counseling before you ever commit to another man. It's only fair to you and to your boyfriend.

Maybe divorce for you is a less serious matter than it was in previous generations. There may be a loss of concern for the Word of God, which emphatically states that only under the cause of adultery should a couple divorce

Many women will divorce because they sense a loss of the passion they once enjoyed with their husband. Passion for each other is important but not essential for the survival of the marriage.

However, in order for most relationships to be considered for further dates and involvement, the potential couple must feel some sense of physical attraction toward each other. The likelihood of a man and woman becoming "an item" without some level of attraction is very small. Research has shown that couples usually had some physical allure for one another when they first met. So the initial passion in the infancy of a relationship should encourage a man and woman to further their relationship.

159

Also, couples seem to be more successful when the man and woman are attracted to each other more-or-less equally. She is as attractive to him as he is handsome to her.

What causes a woman to continue to pursue marriage to a man when she has lost passion for him?

1. She ignores the warning signs.

It is common for women to ignore red flags that warn them that a particular man might not be a good lifelong companion for her. You should pay attention to your gut feelings in assessing men and compatible personalities. Women who have been interviewed for studies on this issue have reflected that they had reservations about marrying their husbands, but they ignored these red flags and/or kept silent.

2. She has too much to lose.

Some women who have dated the same man for quite some time may feel that there's too much invested to turn away from the relationship. Their friends and family are asking when they are going to tie the proverbial knot, the biological clock maybe ticking away, and they have already spent much of their best years together–so why not just marry.

3. Fear of losing face.

There are also those women who fear that walking away from a relationship could result in some accrued embarrassment, and the possibilities of people "talking about her" may be too much for her to emotionally endure. Pressure from others to marry can be quite overwhelming for some women. Family, friends, coworkers, and even her boyfriend could exert an emotional force that will supersede her personal feelings. These women are often people-pleasers and givers in their traits and characteristics. The mantra becomes: "Let's just get married to make everyone happy."

4. It's too hard!

Some want to avoid the complications of breaking up and just make things easier by simply marrying the man. The thought for some ladies to put her boyfriend through the pain of a break up or even a separation may seem intolerable for her. The guilt she may feel on what "she is doing to her boyfriend" maybe inexcusable. So in order to avoid all of this emotional pain, she may agree to the marriage to take the entire burden onto her own shoulders.

5. She has scruples.

For some women find it impendent to marry because of her scruples. You may be in the situation where you have been sleeping with your boyfriend out of wedlock and feel a sense of conviction that this arrangement is wrong in the sight of God. And you would be correct in that thinking. However, you have more than one option. Marrying him is not the only one. There are other possibilities, such as choosing not to be intimate with him any longer. You can also choose not to continue the relationship in spite of your guilt. You do not make fornication right by marrying the man you are sleeping with. You can only make it right by repenting and calling on the forgiveness of God. His forgiveness for all of our sinful actions is every-ready for us!

6. And baby makes three.

If you become pregnant with your boyfriend's child, you may feel forced to provide the baby with the biological father as a family unit. Let me just say up front that you can be a good mother without having to be a wife to a man you are not ready to be married to.

There are myriad reasons why a woman may consider marrying repeatedly. Sometimes a divorce is the result of the man being abusive or a cheater. A woman may feel that continuing the marriage would only put herself and her children in harm's way. Or, she finds it impossible to tolerate being married to married to a man that seeks other women in bed behind her back.

These, and many other reasons that I have not mentioned, lead to divorce and remarriage. It is my hope that you will see that choosing a life partner is not an easy decision. And, that it could be possible you would benefit from the wisdom of spiritual and professional counselors to guide you.

Maybe the option of remaining single should be placed on the table as well. Possibly, after a few to several marriages, you might determine that marriage is just not for you and to remain single will prove to be the best decision you have ever made. Like Paul the apostle, God can give you the grace and strength to be a strong, single woman who cannot only be a great contributor to the church, but also a more attentive mother to your children.

THE UNSUPERVISED WOMAN

Missy's Story

I am an unattractive, middle-aged Texas woman. I know I am unattractive; I can tell. And my husband tells me that I am overweight and ugly anyways, so what's the difference? If my husband thinks I'm ugly, then I'm ugly. He tells me that no one will want me so I'd better stay put in the house with him. I believe him, because I wouldn't want to be married to me either.

But my husband is no looker either. He totally disgusts me with his cussing, his chewing tobacco, his body odor, and his bad breath. I can barely sleep in the same bed with him. He is rough with me in bed, he's abusive to me in front of everyone, and he mocks me even in front of my parents. Sometimes I wish he were dead and gone. I think I would be happier without him. I know that's not Christian-like, but it's always in my mind, especially when he hits me. He pulls my hair and shoves me a lot. It's so humiliating. I wish someone would come in the house and teach him a lesson on how to treat a woman.

THE UNSUPERVISED WOMAN

CHAPTER 10

The Unsupervised Abused Woman

The Unsupervised Abused Woman

"Isn't it sad when you've gotten hurt so much in the past, you can finally say, I'm used to it." **--Unknown**

Woman everywhere are being beaten, kicked, and otherwise abused. These women are all around you – in church, at work, neighbors, family members, and friends. And most of them keep it a secret.

It's hard to fathom, but according to CNN News, 40 percent of American women surveyed reported physical or psychological abuse by their husbands, dates, or boyfriends.

Forty-four percent of women aged 18 to 64 suffer in a "somewhat violent environment" with an intimate partner. Thirteen percent of abused women said the abuse persisted for more than twenty years. Strangely, a battered wife leaves her intimate partner an average of seven times before she gets real help.

Sadly, abuse of women is worse in third-world nations where the cultural standards of domestic violence, battery of women, and psychological abuse are quite different. In 2010, the United Arab Emirates Supreme Court ruled that a man has the right to physically discipline his wife and kids as long as it doesn't leave a mark on their bodies.

According to a UNICEF survey, most believe that a husband is justified in hitting or beating his wife under certain circumstances. Here are some countries and the percentage of their respective population who believe that abusing women should be condoned:

Jordan – 90%
Guinea – 85.6%
Zambia – 85.4%
Sierra Leone – 85%
Laos – 81.2%
Ethiopia – 81%

"It is an epidemic, but it flies under the radar, because of the stigma and shame associated with it. There is also an associated fear that many health care providers have of opening a 'Pandora's Box' of difficult problems that they are unsure how to address." --Dr. Robert Thompson of the Seattle – based Group Health Center for Health Studies.

A woman who has been slapped around, kicked, or otherwise abused is four times more likely to report severe depressive symptoms, and three times more likely to report fair to poor health.

Why would an abused woman put up with the abuse?

1. You may be in denial.

Many abused women refuse to believe that they are actually being abused.

Abused wives may not even recognize that they have a marital problem, let alone abuse.

-Denial keeps abused women locked up – physically and emotionally.

-Denial is a self-destructive coping mechanism.

-Denial is an ill state of mind that is very difficult to break from.

-Denial minimizes the abuse.

-Denial constantly puts the blames on self.

-Denial creates symptoms of depression and low self-esteem.

-Denial can decrease concentration, sleep, or show signs of fatigue.

-Denial exposes women to vulnerability and abuse.

-Denial can cause a woman to burn out emotionally.

-Denial often causes a woman to believe that if she waits long enough, someone will come and rescue her.

2. You may be afraid to leave him.

Fear is the number one reason why a woman will not escape an abusive relationship. She fears for her and her children's lives. Fear is the most telling signal that you are in an abusive relationship. If you feel trepidation, anxiety, caution, and are worried all the time of possible consequences if you disappoint him, then you are certainly in an abusive relationship.

Abusive relationships are like being on an addictive, bad drug. You know that the drug isn't good for you, but you are afraid to come off it because of the withdrawals, detoxing, and side effects. Abuse is very much the same experience. Many women are more afraid of the unknown pain of withdrawing from an abusive partner than the pain of remaining with one.

Spousal abuse is used for one reason–to gain and to maintain total control. Your abuser will not play fair with you. He will use fear, intimidation, and may even hit you.

"I am so ashamed to say this but I am scared to death of my husband. I don't think he will kill me, I know he will. He has killed others. There is nowhere I can hide from him, because he will find me. He is an insane nutcase. He once told me that he would kill my mom and dad first so I would suffer before he killed me." _--T.R.

3. You may lack the resources to leave him.

Often a woman doesn't have the money or the resources in order to live an independent life from her abusive husband or boyfriend – so she stays.

She may have become psychologically and financially dependent upon the abusive husband.

"I have been through hell with someone whom I believe is pathological, as are his whole family. The kids and I, we suffer terribly. He has done the most horrible things to try to break me down. I have to keep strong because I can't get any support from my family and we'd be broke." –W.S.

4. You won't leave because of your children.

A mother will often subjugate herself to abuse for her children's sake. She may fear that she will lose them to her husband in a court battle; she may fear that her children will not fare well without their father living at home with them; or she may fear that her children will suffer financially with her and away from their dad. Often a mother will hide the martial issues from their children so they may blame her for any separation or divorce. It's tough enough to struggle with an abusive man, but it's much more difficult to tolerate him with children in tow.

"I will never let my husband and his family take my kids from me. He says that the courts will award him my kids because I'm crazy and can't afford them. He said he'd hire the biggest barracuda lawyer in town to take the kids and that I will have to pay him child support. I guess I would literally kill myself if that bastard took my kids, so I may as well stay in this mess of a marriage." –O.A.

5. You have feelings of guilt.

You may feel that you deserve the abuse because of some sin or error you may have committed. Or, maybe you feel guilty in leaving your abusive husband all alone to fend for himself. You tell yourself that you still love him, and that you contribute significantly to the fights. As guilt sets in – so you remain.

"He beats me sometimes but I can't leave him. He's pitiful alone; he said he would kill himself if I left him. I cannot have that on my conscience. Everyone will blame me. And then there's our children ..." –G.T.

6. Your man promises to change.

You may be clinging to empty promises of your husband reforming himself. He said he would never talk to you like that or ever hit you again. But hasn't he said that before – time and time again? Men will often say whatever they need to say as long as it results in your not leaving him. It's the "end justifying the means." And in some instances, he may actually mean to get better.

Maybe he has begged and pleaded with you to stay, right after he raged at you and the children. This polarization, that is, shifting from one emotional extreme to another, is typical of abusive men. He starts out with strong intimidation, then when he sees you are going to leave him for that, his emotions go to the opposite pole, to begging and pleading. The problem is that abusive men have difficulty tempering their anger. They do not know how to be angry correctly. They explode, going from zero to one hundred in a second.

"He is just so convincing with his promises to get better. I keep getting sucked into his needs. I am so scared to make the wrong decision, so I just keep taking him back hoping this is the one that's going to change me. The last time he hit me, my ear went deaf. I can now barely hear out of my right ear. After the operation, the doctor told me to be careful with my ear, not to get around loud noises. So I put a piece of cotton in my ear

to filter it. I thought after that, my husband would stop hitting me. He got so scared I would tell someone, but I didn't." –I.P.

7. You see your husband as the strength of your life and family.

You are convinced that he was to be your protector and your provider.

"I knew he was going to be tough to be married to. He had all of these piercings and tattoos and stuff. But I felt so safe with him because he was so scary looking, you know? And he can fight real good, so I know I am safe from anyone trying to mess with me. But I didn't figure he would turn on me.

"He totally withholds any love for me. He never hugs or kisses me. Never says anything nice and never apologizes when he does mean things to me. Isn't he supposed to love on me? I mean, after all, he's my husband. I go to a counselor because of how he treats me. I just want him to take care of me like I see some of my friends' husbands take care of them. Just a kind word every now and then would be so good. Tell me everything is going to be okay. I guess I'm expecting a huge miracle or something." –L.J.

8. You may not leave him because of your religious beliefs.

"We both are Christians, but I can't take him anymore. For the last several years, he's getting worse and worse. He is mean, belittling, and intimidating. He pushed me through a window once, but I don't think he meant to. I trust God and don't believe in divorce, but I need someone to encourage me. Everyone wants me to divorce him, but I think they just want me to be free from his evil ways." -K.B.

9. You stay with him because of unsupportive family and friends.

None of your friends or family believes that your man is abusive. All of your words are ignored. They cannot imagine that that "nice guy" you are so lucky to have is what you are describing to them. So because they don't believe you, you are unable to find any support system to help you or guide you. He may have tarnished your name with lies and slander, so you don't have a chance outside of your husband's house.

"He talks trash about me to everyone, even my friends and mom! He tells everyone I am a slob, that I never cook or clean. He tells them that he does EVERYTHING and I don't do anything around the house. He even told my dad that he found evidence that I have been seeing a guy at work, which is a total lie. Now the guy at work heard about that and he's married. I think I hate my husband for what he has done to me." –N.M.

10. You believe you are responsible for his abusive behavior.

The abuse is your fault, or so you think. Your nagging provoked him into hitting you, right? Many women are unable to place responsibility where is rightly belongs, so they take full responsibility for ever assault, insult, or beating directed toward them. Are you so very brainwashed by incessant blaming that you believe you are at fault?

"I find myself feeling bad for him. I know he can't afford to pay for the house without my paycheck, and he says he's going to kill the dog and cat if I leave him. He says that I am the one that's really the problem. He says what he does to me is not really abuse. I feel like I'm losing my mind. Maybe he's right and I'm the problem, and he's not that bad after all." -S.T.

Every abused spouse needs leverage.
I have learned that people in relationship require some sort of leverage with each other (boundaries) in order to keep a proper balance of honor, love, and respect.

Specifically in abusive cases, every man must clearly see that there are real consequences to his abusive actions. Men usually abuse a woman because "he can." When a man believes that there is nothing or nobody that can stand in his way to abuse a woman physically, mentally, emotionally, or verbally – he is without balance and lacks consequence.

An abused woman must find avenues of consequence that can be leveraged on a man who is treating her wrongly.

-Bring in others for confrontations (police, family, friends, and neighbors).

-Tell others you have been abused (for mediation purposes).

-Call a lawyer to know your rights.

-Separate or divorce depending upon the situation.

-Involve professional counselors.

-Get a restraining order if the abuse calls for it.

-Learn from others in support groups.

-Take a position of self-empowerment.

-Take control over your life—now.

God will take up your cause and your course when you are suffering as the victim. He is an ever-present help to you in the time of trouble to be sure.

"God is our refuge and strength, a very present help in trouble." (Psalm 46:1, King James Version)

He loves you so very much. He is your Savior; not only in your eternal salvation, but also in everything you are a part of on earth. He can save you from your financial plights, your health issues, even from marital discord and abuse. He truly is a Mighty God in all that you do.

"I am He, who will sustain you. I have made you and I will carry you. I will sustain you and rescue you." (Isaiah 46:4 New International Version)

We must come to the shocking reality that we may have people in our lives that are intent on hurting us, and even exterminating us. One of our natural instincts is to run and hide when danger has befallen us. The correct way to hide is in Christ. Hide yourself in Christ Jesus. When we hide in the everlasting and powerful arms of God, there is no one that can do you any harm.

"For in that day of trouble He will keep me safe in His dwelling, He will hide me in the shelter of His tabernacle and

set me on a high rock." (Psalm 27:5, New International Version)

SELAH!

THE UNSUPERVISED WOMAN

SECTION 3:
WOMEN AND THE WORLD

do
not
disturb

THE UNSUPERVISED WOMAN

Harriet's Story

I found myself in a court of law one morning for stealing baby clothes in a popular retail-clothing store. My husband sat beside me; we were both totally humiliated by my actions, though my husband was totally supportive of me. A high-priced lawyer who fortunately knew the judge from prior cases represented me.

The prosecutors, two females, found out that I was a professed Christian, which further humiliated my poor husband and me. As we sat in the courtroom, I watched one of the prosecutors write on a legal pad: "What ever happened to 'Thou shall not steal'!!!" I think she wrote it big so we would be able to read her note to the other prosecutor. I felt like I was dying a thousand deaths sitting there.

I had only stolen $93.00 worth of children's clothes, but it was enough to constitute a felony charge. If I was found guilty, I could be put in jail for quite some time. I was promising God, my husband, and myself, that if He could get me out of this mess I put myself in, that I would never steal again.

I don't have to steal; my husband does well financially. As a matter of fact, we fall into the top two-percentile income bracket, so stealing is a ridiculous risk for me.

As we sat there, which seemed to be years, my lawyer said that he was going to the back to speak to the judge in confidence. We began to pray. He returned, stating that the judge was willing to drop all charges because of the favor he had with the judge. We only had to pay court costs. It was a miracle.

I never stole after that frightening day. But I still want to. God help me.

CHAPTER 11

The Unsupervised Woman Who Steals

The Unsupervised Woman Who Steals

"The only thing worth stealing is a kiss from a sleeping child."
--Joe Houldsworth

Every day, wealthy and respectable women steal merchandise that amounts to millions of dollars a year in retail losses. So says *Woman's Day Magazine,* (January 12, 1993).

In the Woman's Day article, one woman's story really caught my attention:

Katie is a mother of three children, and she has been shoplifting for more than twenty years. It all started when she was a new mother who was bored, restless, and struggling financially. "We hadn't had much money and I had nothing to do but shop," Katie said. The first time she stole was an outfit for her baby daughter. "I just threw it into her carriage and walked right out of the store."

Katie couldn't believe how easy it was, or how good it felt. She said: "It was exciting; I felt great that I'd gotten away with it." A few weeks later, she found herself stealing again. At first it was a game, but she soon found that she couldn't stop playing. Money had stopped being an issue a long time ago, but the shoplifting remained a problem for her.

This story describes the situation of many women who keep a secret lifestyle that is as addictive as any drug one might take. Some of the most famous celebrities steal, even though they have more than enough money to purchase the merchandise.

Some of the most famous celebrities suffer from kleptomania, (a stealing mental disorder) even though they have more than enough money to purchase the merchandise they take. Lindsay Lohan was caught stealing a necklace; Winona Ryder was caught stealing large amounts of merchandise from Saks Fifth Avenue; Jennifer Capriati, a tennis prodigy, was caught stealing a ring. Even pop star Britney Spears, who is worth over one hundred million dollars, was apprehended stealing a lighter, a wig, and a $200.00 blouse. A famous young British model, Peaches Geldof, was caught stealing a $500.00 dress and had several other stealing altercations. Farrah Fawcett was arrested twice for shoplifting clothes from two different stores. The daughter of former New York mayor Rudy Giuliani was arrested for stealing $150.00 worth of cosmetics. The actress Megan Fox stole a $7.00 tube of lipstick. And Bess Myerson, former Miss America, was caught shoplifting as well.

Most women who shoplift are more often than not guilty of stealing small items that range from clothing to makeup and jewelry. Ironically, however, a woman in England was arrested while attempting to sneak out of the store with a 42-inch television under her dress, between her legs. She actually got completely out of the store before she was apprehended.

Anonymous Confessions of Female Shoplifters:

"I steal more than I'd like to admit."

"I steal useless stuff all the time. I'm guessing over $5,000.00 worth of useless stuff. I have a criminal record now and a job that pays hardly anything. It's because my stealing stole my life."

"It's the adrenaline rush. I work in security, and I still can't help it. Every time I do it, I risk losing my job. But it's an addiction I can't quit."

"OMG! I never get caught stealing. It's just too easy."

"I stole five bras--all under my clothes. They were so pretty and so expensive. And thank God they didn't have security tags on them."

"I steal all the time. Hundreds of dollars' worth."

"I steal small things all the time from my friends. I borrow stuff and I never give it back to them. I don't know why I do it."

"I steal about $1500.00 worth of clothing, makeup, and jewelry every week."

* (Much of the information in this section was acquired from The National Association of Shoplifters Prevention – NASP – www.nasp.org)

"I'm addicted to stealing. When I don't steal, I get mad because I know I can get away with it without paying. I like stealing because I will have something new to wear the next day."

-"When I steal I usually buy something too, so I don't feel too bad."

So why would you or any good women steal? *

1. Maybe you are substituting for a loss in your life.

"Put no trust in extortion, set no vain hopes on robbery; if riches increase, set not your heart on them." (Psalm 62:10, English Standard Version)

Even though many good women are generally decent, honest citizens, something might have happened in their past—

some kind of deprivation—such as divorce, serious illness, death of a loved one, loss of income or career, loss of investments, or even unexpected expenses, that triggered the desire to steal. Have you ever experienced a loss in your life that has led you to shoplifting and stealing?

2. Maybe you feel that you deserve a justifiable payback.

"Let the thief no longer steal ..." (Ephesians 4:28, English Standard Version)

Women who feel they live their lives giving of all they have to give, until they can't give anymore, often turn to stealing. Some feel justified in taking what isn't theirs as a means of "payback" to compensate for the lack of reciprocation. These women are nurturing by nature and have a heart to provide for everyone. They may have taken on the bulk of the responsibility to provide for their family to the point where they try to justify taking (stealing) whatever their family needs. Do you feel that you have given away so much of yourself that you deserve a payback or a return on all of your expended time and treasure?

3. Maybe you are experiencing a relief mechanism.

Many women steal to release frustration, anxiety, boredom, and depression. These women often have an unresolved mourning, feelings of loss, or high stress levels. These women often have a rage factor, which seems to subside when they shoplift. Women who steal to substitute for a feeling of loss feel a sense of shame when they shoplift. One woman testified that she would rather have been addicted to alcohol rather than stealing. At least alcoholism is treated with some empathy. But stealing is treated with aggression, name-calling, and even withdrawal by those who fear being a victim of their loved one's stealing. Do you feel that you are ready to explode with frustration and anxiety, and that the only release is to experience the feelings brought on by stealing or shoplifting?

4. Maybe you are suffering from depression and you feel better when you steal.

Studies show that one third of the women who shoplift and steal suffer from some type of depression and melancholy. Actually, depression as a mental illness is the common denominators found among women who steal and shoplift that really don't have to for financial reasons. This also may explain why many good women steal on their birthdays and holidays. The rate of female shoplifters in mental hospitals is three times as high as the rate of general hospital admissions. Do you see a connection between your shoplifting/stealing and any signs of depression in your life?

5. Are you self-indulgent? Do you feel entitled to the merchandise?

"Treasures gained by wickedness do not profit..." (Proverbs 10:2, English Standard Version)

When a poor woman steals, she's called a common thief. When a well-to-do woman steals, she's called a deviant. Some women feel that they are entitled to the better things in life and should not have to pay for it. It's the belief that you should get something for nothing. These women are self -indulgent, thrill seekers who enjoy taking risks, love challenges, and find stealing fun. They may even see shoplifting as a type of revenge. They may diffuse their responsibility and blame the store or another person for forcing them to steal the merchandise. One study showed that a certain type of woman would find sexual satisfaction from being caught in that act of thievery–self-serving at its very core. Do you feel entitled to merchandise that you have not paid for? Have you convinced yourself that others owe things to you and shouldn't charge you for them?

Is the feeling of entitlement reserved just for bad or needy people? Are there any practicing religious women who also feel entitled to steal, rob, or shoplift as well? There was a headline not too long ago that read: "Hasidic Women Shoplift at Talbots." This newspaper article said that Hasidic women have "sticky fingers." The owner of the store was quoted as saying: "We love it when the sun goes down on Friday until sundown on Saturday– it's their Sabbath and they have to be home by sunset. So we don't have to be monitoring them every second."

Evidently these ultra-conservative Jewish women, all dressed in heavily wrapped, Middle Eastern garb, felt that stealing from retailers was an entitlement for them in spite of the what the Ten Commandments state, or what the Pentateuch demands: "Thou shall not steal." They may feel this law doesn't apply to them if they are stealing from a non-Hasidic or those who are not in their particular religion.

6. Do you feel that you get a rush or high from stealing or shoplifting?

The excitement generated from getting away with stealing, thievery, or shoplifting produces a chemical reaction, which results in what many women describe as a rush or a high. Many females will confess that the true reward is not having the merchandise but rather the act of stealing, which gives them the rush. Some shoplifters who are addicted to stealing describe their addiction to the rush or high as commensurate with the addiction of drugs or alcohol. Do you feel that there is a personal inner pressure for you to steal? Would you compare that feeling to those who crave an illicit drug?

7. Maybe being caught does not frighten you.

There are actually 27 million shoplifters in America today, which amounts to 35 million dollars a day stolen from retailers. That's one in eleven Americans who steals daily. And shoplifters are caught once in every forty-eight theft attempts. An average shoplifter steals an average of 1.8 times a week. So, it makes sense that he or she will eventually be caught.

The law of averages will catch up to you if you are shoplifting, and it will prove to be a most embarrassing time for you if you are prosecuted. Your name might be printing in the local paper; you may be charged with a felony, be forced to do community service, fined, and put in jail. The court and attorney costs will be a big expense. Does getting caught frighten you? Research has shown that many women feel that they are too smart to ever be caught. They also believe that if caught, they will get off without being charged with a crime. Do you see that this logic is abnormal for a good citizen?

How to get help

It's possible that for you to stop stealing and shoplifting, some rough events that have severe consequences must take place, like arrest, fines, jail time, and community service. Maybe having your name printed in the local newspaper for shoplifting will shame you into changing. I truly hope it never comes to this for you.

There are many group therapy programs, treatment centers, and prevention programs, not to mention self-help books, church assistance programs, counseling, even sharing your plight with your minister, which can put you on the path to stopping this compulsion.

I truly understand that in order for you to stop stealing, it's going to take a lot of prayer, self-discipline, will power, and a personal commitment to make these important changes. But you can do it.

Here are some pointers that may help you in your quest to stop stealing:

-Avoid stores that have very poor or lax security systems.

-Shop only when necessary. Make a list of the things that you are going to buy before you leave your house. Go to the store and buy only those items; then get out of the store.

-Totally shun window-shopping and browsing; it's far too tempting.

-Do not wear big coats or clothing that has large pockets. Try to wear tight- fitting clothing so you do not have any place to hide merchandise on your person.

-Carry a clutch handbag just large enough to fit your keys and wallet.

-If at all possible, bring a friend along.

-If you begin to feel the urge to steal, or you begin to see the possibilities of getting away with shoplifting, remove yourself from the store. Come back later when the temptation has subsided.

-Get involved with a church group. Go to church services as often as you can. Volunteer at the church to keep you around Christians and Christian activities.

Some of the nicest, kindest, Christian women suffer from kleptomania.

Woman who do not have to steal or shoplift for financial reasons are ensnared by an addiction that is very difficult to break away from. Many of these women lead a very secret life because of their thievery. They are usually ashamed of themselves, and dare not tell anyone for fear of intolerable judgment.

As the woman depicted on the cover of this book who appears to be hiding behind a slightly opened door, you may be suffering from a force or obsession to steal or shoplift. There is help for you if you will only seek it out. God knows that you are suffering with this torment, so give it over to Him to heal you. Remember, many of our sins are merely our weaknesses and not wickedness.

Tammy's Story

I have been having a very intense relationship with this amazing man for two years now. We want to get married; but we are not in any hurry. It's a crazy relationship; he likes everything that I like. He's the perfect guy for me and he tells me that I am the perfect woman for him. I have only one small problem: we have only communicated by Facebook.

We have never seen one another. Don't get me wrong; we talk on the phone all the time. He doesn't have Skype so we can't do the face-to-face thing yet.

But I cannot wait to meet him. He is heavenly. My friends and family thinks he is not who he says he is, and that he might be a woman or something worse. But I know him so well like I know myself, so I'm not listening to them. I am going to believe positive things and not torment myself thinking that he is lying to me. If he isn't the man who he tells me he is, I don't know what I would do.

It's not that my family is just being evil to me or jealous. They just don't understand why he can't meet me. I tell them that he's real busy travelling with his job and stuff. He says he won't Skype because he wants our first meeting to be memorable and not cheapened by the computer screen. I think that is so romantic.

My family will see one day that I was right to trust my man. And he is going to be all and more that he says he is.

Jessica's Story

I have been leading a man on with a make-believe Facebook profile for almost a year now. And it's getting to the point that he's totally fallen in love with me and I with him. This is real bad because I am not the woman in the photos I sent him, nor am I a lot of things I told him I was. It's just that he is so dreamy and I am not. If the truth were told, I am an overweight woman and he's a lean, mean-machine hunk of a man. He wouldn't look twice at me if he knew what I really looked like. But now he knows my heart and the beauty I have on the inside. Now all of the personal stuff I tell him is all for real. I don't lie about myself, and what my life is all about. It's only the photos that are not me. I took a bunch of pictures from a gallery book of this insanely beautiful model and posed them as me on my false profile.

I realize that I am in deep ... you know what. He's in love with a face that's not mine. I am trying to lose weight like crazy, but to look like the pictures I sent to him, I'd have to lose over a hundred pounds. I was thinking that I could drop the weight, color and cut my hair like the pictures, but the plan isn't going so well. He is going to get so hurt. I wish I could just tell him the truth though, but I don't want to lose him. My sister told me that I never actually had him, and that he's in love with a fictitious woman. But I told her that everything I told him was really me, it's just the pictures that are fake.

No matter how I play this through in my mind, something tells me it's not going to end well. I will lose him, and I will be heart-broken. I guess so will he. I'm just going to communicate with him as long as I can before he catches me.

CHAPTER 12

The Unsupervised Woman with Fake Facebook Profiles

THE UNSUPERVISED WOMAN

The Unsupervised Woman with Fake Facebook Profiles

"He was smoking hot, too good to be true, and can you believe it, he was interested in me!" --**Victim of a Facebook member with a false profile**

If you haven't heard of Facebook, you may have been hiding under a rock these past few years. Facebook is the largest social network site in the world, and it is fast becoming the cupid of dating. Actually, Facebook is rivaling professional dating online services such as Harmony.com and Match.com because of the free vetting that is available on Facebook.

However, according to CNN reports, 83 million Facebook accounts are fakes and dupes, and one in four users lie on their personal profiles. According to Facebook statistics, there are 4,704 mentions per month of fake profiling—that's 6.53 reports of false identities per hour. And that's only the ones that are being caught. No telling how many false identities and profiles are actually out there saying they are someone they are not. One woman recently wrote: "I have over 500 false Facebook accounts for various reasons that I don't want to say." I believe that people who lie on their profiles range from those who are doing it innocently to those who have malicious intent.

"The heart is deceitful above all things, and desperately sick; who can understand it?" (Jeremiah 17:9, English Standard Version)

On Facebook (and other similar social networking sites) you can casually meet new people, hunt for potential mates, strike up a conversation or a chat, send an instant message, send a private message, establish that you are of single status, poke with flirtations, and photo share. You can search for past lovers as far back as grade school, monitor boyfriends, share feelings and emotions, and feel a general sense of belonging to the rest of society.

The malicious side of Facebook

Countless men, women, and even kids falsify their Facebook profiles with ill intent in order to prey upon, to hurt, and to offend others. And there are myriad ways to hurt and cause misery to someone on Facebook, especially those who are vulnerable and unsuspecting. These predators are false investors, stalkers, bullies, blackmailers, identity thieves, voyeurs, and impersonators specializing in hoaxing and punking, larceny, posing, slandering, incriminating, hacking, profaning, exposing private photos and videos of others, property theft, stolen identities, phishing attacks, impersonating, obsessions, exhibitionism and flashing, revenge, teasing, insulting and harassing.

"While evil men and impostors will go from bad to worse, deceiving and being deceived." (2 Timothy 3:13, New International Version)

And many of these malicious profilers can prove to be serious psychos and sickos that are bent on ruining your life and the lives of your family members and friends. They are called pick-up hacks, pick-up grifters, pick-up blackmailers, pick-up extortionists, and the old-fashioned pick-up artists.

The potential evils of false Facebook profiling, especially in romantic relationships, has become so notorious that a reality show has been totally dedicated to finding the truthful origins of Facebookers who pose as an online lover to a hopeful and naïve someone.

Nev Schulman created Catfish an MTV program that brings the watching audience through his investigations in hopes of exposing romantic dupers to the forefront. Schulman has been successful in bringing many Facebook romantics into the same room physically for the first time–and with mixed results.

Once a genuine lover has gotten so frustrated in wanting to meet his or her online counterpart, they can call on Schulman to investigate and hopefully arrange a meeting between the lovers. Most of the episodes expose the mysterious lover as a fraud. Fraudulent lovers are often of the same sex as the victim, or a minor, and never match the picture depicted on their profile. Most of the time, the profile photos are randomly chosen pictures of very attractive men and women. The frauds are often grossly overweight, unattractive, or some mixture of both. There are also the rare occasions where the fraudulent lover is actually a friend of the unsuspecting lover, and for various reasons, carries on a fantasy relationship with him or her.

When the Catfish producers and Nev Schulman bring the two lovers together, there is often great heartbreak, shock, feelings of betrayal and even anger. I must confess as a member of the watching audience, that it's heart wrenching to watch the two online lovers meet for the first time, and witnessing the shock of seeing who the fraud really turns out to be. The meeting can be explosive.

For diverse reasons, many Facebook lovers carry on their love affairs strictly online. Many have never seen one another face-to-face or even on Skype. For some of these romantics, they will continue literally for years, communicating only in Facebook chat rooms, by instant messaging, personal messages, a few photos exchanged, and maybe an occasional phone call, but never to meet in the flesh.

So why would you create a false Facebook profile?

For the most part, women who pose or impersonate more attractive people than themselves are unhappy women looking for an escape—even if it's just for a while. They may enjoy the feeling of being someone else for a change. It may cause them to feel pretty, wanted, needed, loved, and belonging to someone who in reality—in the flesh—could never be. You feel that if the man you are dating online knew what you really looked like, he would never give you a second thought. Right?

1. Do you feel you are overweight or unattractive?

Are you posing as a skinny, attractive model of a woman in order to ignore, just for a while, your overweight and unattractive self (well, at least that's how you perceive yourself)?

You know that these fantasy relationships are shallow and unreal, and someone is going to get emotionally hurt by your secret. If you will notice the cover artwork of this book, you may see yourself hiding behind that slightly ajar door, living a secret life, posing as another woman, and hurting inside.

I suppose that most of the women who pose as attractive, model-like specimens of a female are overweight. And sadly, these women have no hope of seeing themselves as thin, attractive, or wanted. So, for them, it is a pleasure to converse with a Greek-god of a man who has opened up his heart and soul on Facebook, or even on the phone. I would suggest to you not to give up on yourself. If you are truly overweight, you can lose the pounds necessary to get you healthy and more satisfying in appearance. But please know that attractiveness does not ensure a happy relationship. Indeed, beauty is truly on the inside of all of us.

2. *Maybe you've been the good woman, but want to be the bad woman.*

Did you create a new life as a naughty woman—teasing and flirting, and maybe even releasing a suppressed rage, all from a safe distance of a false Facebook profile? Did you create a relationship with someone that exchanges sexual fantasies with you, and lead him on as if the two of you will meet some day? Maybe you thought that by merely changing your profile, you could harmlessly pose as a totally different person. But have you considered the consequences of such a relationship?

"Let us not become weary in doing good, for at the proper time we will reap a harvest if we do not give up." (Galatians 6:9, New International Version)

Maybe the man you are leading on is being truthful and honest with you, and he may have fallen in love with someone who doesn't exist. This can be so harmful to him, even if your intentions were good. This web of deceit that you have woven has been accomplished with just a click of your mouse. It may have started out as a funny project in order to engage a man with a sensual side of you, but it's wrong.

3. Maybe you are a femme fatale.

Do you get a rush by deceiving people? Is enticing a man for his money, time, and even his very soul exciting for you? Do you pose as a hot Asian girl desperately needing financial help? Are you impersonating a poor Russian woman who needs money so you can rendezvous with him? Or are you targeting a specific person who has hurt you, so you are seeking revenge? Do you lead him on by claiming you will provide fantastic sexual favors for him?

"Lying lips are an abomination to the Lord, but those who act faithfully are his delight." (Proverbs 12:22, English Standard Version)

I must say, that for all the reasons that women may impersonate a Facebook profile, being an online predator is, in my opinion, the cruelest intentions of all. Words that come to my mind that would describe an online femme fatale are: devious, cruel and evil, plotting and scheming, thievery, and opportunistic—just to name a few. Many of the men that entertain your deceptions are often lonely, simplistic, gullible, and naïve. And I would suppose that the men who are possibly sending you money are not financially well to do.

"For God will bring every deed into judgment with every secret thing, whether good or evil." (Ecclesiastes 12:14, English Standard Version)

A femme fatale also encourages men to engage in perverse communication, and potentially opens these men into an illicit life of sexually deviant pursuits such as pornography, voyeurism, and sinful conversations.

4. Maybe you are married and dissatisfied with your husband.

"It's easy to deny an emotional affair, but it can be extremely threatening to a marriage." Dr. Gail – MSNBC

Did you make up a Facebook account in order to emotionally cheat on your husband? Maybe you wanted some cheap thrills in your life by falsifying a Facebook profile in order to bring in some forbidden romance (that you don't seem to get from your husband). But it's cruel to engage someone in a relationship that leads a man on as if he has a chance to be with you in the future. You probably do not intend to leave your husband and family, so the man you are facebooking is probably going to be hurt by your lies.

Have you been the target of a Facebook impersonator?

"They are the kind that worm their way into homes and gain control over weak-willed women..." (2 Timothy 3:6, New International Version)

I am sorry that you have been lied to in a Facebook relationship. I do not know what damage may have been done or what the fabricated relationship may have cost you; whether it was the loss of emotions, trust, and love, maybe your monetary savings, maybe great humiliation, or maybe even all of the above. Truly, my heart goes out to you.

"For such men are slaves, not of our Lord Christ, but of their own appetites; by their smooth and flattering speech they deceive the hearts of the unsuspecting." (Romans 16:18, New International Version)

If this false relationship has caused you to isolate yourself and not trust anymore, I would ask you to turn to Jesus Christ who will heal your broken heart and return to you all that was destroyed and robbed from you.

"I will restore to you the years that the locust hath eaten ..." (Joel 2:25, King James Version)

If you have an interest in investigating a Facebook friend whom you suspect might be using a false profiles, I can suggest several ways to determine whether this person is legitimate or not.

Ten Ways to Catch a Fake Facebook Profiler

-If he looks too good to be true, then he's probably too good to be true.

-Be suspicious of all profile photos and picture galleries.

-If he avoids phone calls, Skyping, meetings in the flesh, or picture updates - then he's probably duping you.

-If he only has female "friends," then he may not be a man.

-If the account is new, then it may be a fake.

-If he has very few friends – he may be targeting you or someone else.

-If he's not conversing between specific friends, but seems to only generate arbitrary statements to all of his friends, then the account maybe fraudulent.

-Send personal messages to his friends to see if they have ever physically met him, and if so, ask if the profile picture is really him.

-If his pictures seem to be model-like poses, then it's probably not him.

-If he tells you where he works – call him at his jobsite or office.

If you are a woman who is impersonating another woman on your Facebook account, please reconsider. As we have discussed in this chapter, posing as someone you are not is harmful to all parties involved. When you have become content with yourself, and found value in who you really are, then you can pursue a healthy and transparent relationship.

You are a beloved and highly favored woman of God. He has great and marvelous plans for you. But the plans for you are actually for the real you – not some fabricated facsimile of yourself.

"For I know the plans I have for you, declares the Lord, plans to prosper you and not harm you, plans to give you hope and a future." (Jeremiah 29:11, New International Version)

Sonya's Story

I never had any interest in watching pornography. It was my husband's idea to watch porn together. He said it would spice up our sex life. Well, I didn't want him to be sneaking around watching porn on his own or even trying to find someone who would please him better than I could. So I said OK to it.

We watched pornography until one or both of us became aroused and we tried to imitate what we were seeing others do on the videos. To say it got out of hand is an understatement. We started to do bad things until we realized that porn was actually damaging our marriage rather than spicing it up. So we agreed to stop. After all, we both are Christians and are very active in our local church we attend.

The down side was that I began to visit the porn sites on my own when my husband wasn't home. I found myself visiting sites several times a day in between cleaning the house and picking up the kids at school. It was getting out of hand for me, but I was really enjoying it sexually. I feel bad saying that, but it was true. I had all the guilt and shame that came with it after I would watch sex online, but it wasn't enough to stop me. I kept saying that this was going to be the last time – but it wasn't. I wanted to tell my husband or my best girlfriend, but I was too scared or ashamed to tell anyone.

The alarm really went off when I began to get into some sites that were very off center--very perverted and dark. It was scaring me. So I began to pray to God for help to get me out of this addiction. I wanted to throw the computer away, but my family uses it regularly. They would ask me why I got rid of it, and I would have to lie to them. They'd just buy another one anyway.

One day in church, the pastor was preaching about getting deliverance, and even mentioned pornography. Though it was obvious he was referring to the men in the audience, I knew that that was me. I certainly couldn't go up to the altar and tell a prayer partner, because I feared she would tell someone. So I went to the altar alone and gave the addiction to God. I felt a sense of relief like a blowing of fresh wind through me. I knew right then and there that I had victory over pornography. Now, it's not that I don't get tempted, and I know that this story may not work for everyone, but for me, it was my saving grace out of that darkness.

CHAPTER 13

The Unsupervised Porn-addicted Woman

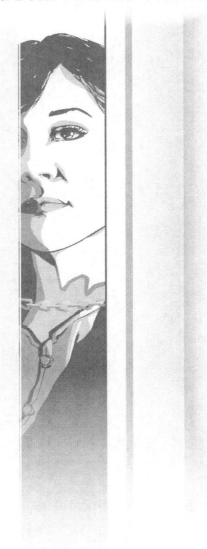

The Unsupervised Porn-addicted Woman

"A widespread taste for pornography means that nature is alerting us to some threat of extinction. --J.G. **Ballard**

"What porn is really about, ultimately, isn't sex but death." --**Susan Sontag**

"It was like opening up a door from hell. I opened this door to darkness and debauchery. All of these demons came in. It was a secret sin that had me, and I could not shake it loose. It had me at the throat because it had me at the very heart. It was taking over my very life, and it was snuffing out the life of Christ in me. It choked the Word and prayer out of my life."

This is the testimony of Joean, a porn addicted, Christian woman, (as reported by Zsa Zsa Palagyi of the 700 Club). Joean started buying pornography videos from pawnshops, and she went to enormous efforts to hide her secret, shameful addiction. She purchased the videos, then painstakingly peeled off the title labels and hid the videos under the front seat of her car. Once everyone in her family was asleep, she would watch the videos. The next morning, she would put the video into a brown paper bag and trash it at work.

Joean was a devoted Christian and even spoke at large groups about her belief in God and her faith. Sadly, she had a secret life that she could not share with anybody. She was addicted to pornography as intensely as a drug addict is addicted to drugs.

According to Tanith Cary, a writer for the Guardian, 17 percent of women describe themselves as addicted to porn. And although pornography addiction typically is seen as a man's problem, increasing numbers of women admit to being addicted to Internet pornography. Many of these women are revealing that porn addiction is leaving them in despair and loneliness. Pornography addiction is fast becoming an unspoken struggle among the female gender.

Psychotherapist Phillip Hodson says, "Women habitually using porn is something that has never been aired before. It's something new that's just beginning to surface. Traditionally, women's voices have been against porn. It seems more of a man thing, because men are supposed to be visually stimulated. But that doesn't mean that women aren't. Men are just maybe more so."

Even the Washington Times writer Rachel Duke wrote: "One out of every six women surveyed, including Christian women, acknowledged that they struggled with pornography." Christian women are not safe from the influences and addictive nature of pornography.

Some startling statistics on women using pornography*

-One out of every three porn sites is viewed by women.

-30 percent of porn consumers are women.

-9.4 million women access adult websites every month.

-13 percent of women admit that they visit porn sites at their workplace.

-Internet porn has become increasingly attractive to women because of anonymity and safety.

-Women are especially attracted to adult chat rooms so they can act out sexually in a relationship that is not real.

*(Internet Pornographic Statistics)

Why are women becoming increasingly interested in pornography?

1. Women are revealing that pornography can be used as way to have sex without all the emotional involvement. For these women, the appeal is the sexual experience without all of the complications that relationships require. You actually don't have to deal with a real person while using online porn – it's all

very impersonal and void of romantic feelings. The trouble with this logic is that many women sadly find it difficult to be intimate because of addiction to pornography.

2. Women are finding that porn has that instant gratification on their body and mind. Internet porn is the "ways and means" of getting sexual pleasures real quick and easy. Porn removes the need for a woman to prepare for sex with a man, such as, showering, bathing, shaving, primping, curling, perfuming, sexy lingerie, and brushing her teeth. Women have admitted that they will visit a porn site at work, on the run, and even visit up to twenty sites in a twenty-four hour period.

3. Women are also discovering that there is no fear of poor sexual performance. With Internet porn, there is no need to worry if their boyfriend or husband has been satisfied, or whether he enjoyed her participation, or fear that her body will be unattractive to him. There is no rejection factor for her with pornography.

4. For young girls, there is a safety factor. There is no fear of violation, kidnapping, abductions, pregnancies, broken virginity, break ups, separations, or abuse. A young girl has no worries that her boyfriend will tell others in the school that she slept with him, thereby giving her a potentially bad reputation.

5. Many girls may feel that pornography is a great way to become educated in sexual acts so as not to be ignorant on her

honeymoon night. Girls and women alike may use pornography as an education tool to better please their mate. Sadly, however, this educational tool often becomes a full-blown addiction. And pornography is not an accurate education, as the actors are "acting"; the relation to reality is extremely skewed.

6. Some women may feel that sex with pornography is more pleasurable than with a man, because she knows her body much better than any man does. It can be quite frustrating to a woman who has a male partner who doesn't have a clue how to satisfy her sexually. Countless women have reported to the Shere Hite surveys that they are inclined to fake orgasms because their husbands don't understand the female erogenous zones.

7. Some women may be in a relationship where she feels she cannot have sex with her mate because of lack of attraction, lack of compatibility, or loss of love and confidence. Sadly, many marriages are so weakened by family responsibilities and commitments that passion has been lost at the expense of work and children. Often husbands and wives let themselves go physically. There may be a lack of concern to be intimate because of exhaustion, or even a lack of respect and security toward each other.

8. There are women who are married to husbands who are not capable of having sex because of physical or psychological impediments. The man may have been injured, or is experienc-

ing erectile dysfunction, impotency, prostate issues, loss of testosterone, or taking medications that impede sexual performance, or have psychological issues that makes intimacy impossible.

9. There are single women who want to have sex but do not want to sleep with any man who is not her husband. She feels that she cannot rightfully fornicate or commit adultery, so sadly she uses pornography to satisfy herself.

10. Some women have been violated and cannot feel safe in an intimate relationship with a man, but may find pornography a safe way to enjoy sex without worrying about having flashbacks of violations.

11. Maybe her interest in pornography has graduated to addiction and she feels that she cannot stop.

What complications are women having with pornography?

Some women find their body saying yes to the pleasures they find in the porn, but their mind is telling them no—that it is wrong. And because of this moral conflict, women experience depression and low self-esteem as they regularly visit these illicit adult sites. So it's difficult for such women to reconcile these inner conflicts of enjoyment versus their conscience that stands against the experience of porn. But as they become frequent users of pornographic sites, they become caught up in the addiction that comes with regular usage. So they continue to visit these sites more often because of the addiction at a great cost—the loss of a conscience. When we at first commit an act of immorality, we initially feel a great sense of sadness. However, once a person continues to commit the same act repeatedly, the intensity of this wrongdoing becomes less impressive.

Crystal Renaud, the author of the book *Dirty Girls Come Clean,* wrote that she was a Christian girl of eleven years old when she saw pornography for the first time. Renaud said that she became addicted to porn from that day on. And her addiction would last for the next eight years.

She said she had no friends or passions and that she had only one mission in life–to watch pornography. She writes: "Porn. Masturbation. Cybersex. Webcam sex. Anything you could think up, I watched, experienced and enjoyed. No matter how many times I would say I would stop, I would just keep doing it."

So many things can adversely affect you when you are habitually watching porn:

-*Pornography dulls the mind; it's hollow and unsatisfactory.*

-Pornography makes you anxious and frustrated.

-Pornography isolates you from friends and family.

-Pornography increases the importance of sex without emotions.

-Pornography keeps a woman in a state of guilt and shame.

-Pornography sets sexual expectations in unrealistic scenarios.

-Pornography makes sex with your husband appear dull or mundane.

What are some steps that you can take to help you stop watching pornography?

The most important step in helping yourself stop watching porn is to confess to a friend or family member that you are addicted to pornography, and that you need their help. Becoming transparent to someone and becoming accountable to her or him is the beginning of your detachment from this addiction. You can refer to this close person as your accountability partner. Give him or her access to all of your passwords, download history, iPhone, iPad, and other electronic device information. Several types of blocks can be put onto your smart devices that can prevent any pornographic material from getting to you. You can also arrange to send all of your computer activity to your partner automatically through these downloads and software. Your partner will see whatever you are viewing.

Another change you can make in your life to help you avoid pornography is to rearrange you daily schedule to insure that you are never alone with your electronics. Don't stay home alone if at all possible. Try to be with people as much as you can. Reschedule your daily habits to ensure that you're not constantly looking for opportunities to get alone with your computer. You may begin to feel irritable or anxious because your addiction will cry out to you, but if you stay true to yourself, pray for strength, and avoid alone times–you can break this bad habit.

If you are a woman who travels frequently, try to bring a friend or family member with you. If that isn't possible or practical, leave your laptop, iPad, and other electronics at home. If that is not feasible, try to share a hotel room with a coworker. Travelling adults are often morally challenged when they find themselves alone in a hotel room with a television that provides adult entertainment. Saleswomen, airline attendants, businesswomen who are required to be in many different locations in order to conduct their business activities, often have a lot of spare time in between appointments. If you have this challenge, try to visit the local scenery, take in the sites, research the local history, window shop in the local shopping centers and malls, take in a church service in the area, and get good and tired for a sound sleep. Be sure to have a structured prayer life and Bible reading each day.

Another step for you to take in defeating pornographic addiction is to discipline your mind as Paul the Apostle has said:

"For though we walk in the flesh, we do not war after the flesh: (for our weapons of warfare are not carnal, but mighty through God to the pulling down of strongholds;) casting down imaginations ... and bringing every thought to the obedience of Christ." (2 Corinthians 10:3-5, King James Version)

Although mastering the control of your imaginations and thoughts may seem impossible for you, Paul says it's well within your ability in Christ Jesus. It is pertinent to study how Satan will attempt to tempt you to pornography by putting thoughts and imaginations into your mind. Our role is not only to catch Satan putting ideas into our heads, but also to pull them down and neutralize them in the Holy Ghost.

One way of neutralizing illicit thoughts is to think on other things that are more edifying.

"Finally, brothers, whatever is true, whatever is noble, whatever is right, whatever is pure, whatever is lovely, whatev-

er is excellent or praiseworthy – think about such things." (Philippians 4:8, New International Version, 1984)

It is so important to fill your mind with good and wholesome thoughts and discipline your mind to filter out imaginations that lead to immorality and filthiness.

Sometimes it requires drastic measures on your part to break a pornographic habit.

Jesus talked extensively in the Bible about lusting after the flesh, committing fornication, and adultery. He told His adherers that adultery is actually committed when a person lusts after another person, even shy of physical contact. Jesus, on a few occasions, instructed His followers about the need to become serious about things that are in their lives that cause them to spiritually stumble.

"If your right eye causes you to sin, gouge it out and throw it away. It is better for you to lose one part of your body than for your whole body to be thrown into hell. And if your right hand causes you to sin, cut it off and throw it away. It is better for you to lose one part of your body than for your whole body to go to hell." (Matthew 5:29-30, New International Version, 1984)

These are drastic words by Jesus that demand drastic action on our part in order to avoid being thrown into hell. Thank

God, Jesus was using analogies here; we should not take Him literally. Can you imagine having to chop off your right hand or pluck out your right eye if it is causing you to sin?

But there is a huge lesson here for those who will listen. Maybe computers are not meant for some of us. It is possible that many women need to rethink owning smart devices because the temptation to view pornography is too intense.

Let's take some poetic license here and replace some of the words in the Scriptures in Matthew 5:29-30:

If your computer causes you to sin, throw it out. It is better for you to lose a computer than for you to sin. If your iPad or Smart Phone offends you, throw them out, for it is better for you to lose the electronics than for you to sin.

I realize that it may be impractical to throw away your electronics, especially when the family uses them, or you require them for work. However, if you clearly see that drastic action should be taken in your life, you should seriously consider it, even if just for a season.

I once witnessed a man heaving a beautiful television into a dumpster one afternoon. Another onlooker asked if the television was working. The man replied that it was virtually a new TV! The onlooker asked if he could take the TV home with him. The man said he didn't mind. Once the onlooker walked off with the television, I inquired as to why he was throwing a working TV into the dumpster. He said that the TV was killing his family. He turned into a couch potato and watched cable shows that were pornographic. His wife was addicted to soap operas, the kids were addicted to cartoons, and there was absolutely no family time for them together. They all agreed as a family that for the next twelve months, they would go without a TV.

I bumped into this man some months later, and I asked how things were going without the TV. He said, "At first it was awkward; we didn't know what to do with ourselves. We actually thought we'd made a big mistake. Then things started to get better. We began to sit at the table together for meals. We had great family discussions, and we played board games together. Then we started a home group in our house with friends from our church. It's the best thing we have ever done for our family. I doubt we will replace the TV."

You have the God-given ability to defeat this habit!

An increasing number of women have been snared into the dark world of pornography. Large percentages of women around the nation are coming forth and admitting that they have an addiction to adult porn sites.

Sadly, pornography is no respecter of persons, even among Christian women. But there is divine assistance we all can rely on through the Holy Spirit who comforts and directs us in the way we should go. The Holy Spirit is a great influence in Christians lives. The Spirit inhabits you as a house, speaks to your spirit to do righteously, intercedes for you in your battles, and provides gifts and fruits to you that are supernatural abilities to live a holy life.

Why not start today? Right now. Find a friend or family member to confide in. Take steps to avoid "alone time" with smart electronics. Become accountable to someone. Recreate your environment so it can be porn free. Attend as many church services as possible through the week, and most importantly, pray for God to deliver you from the snares of pornography.

CONCLUSION

Conclusion

Your secret is not a secret to God.

Everything you do, say, think, imagine, contemplate, plot, scheme, desire, hurt, and suffer is all known to God. He knows your frame and limitations, and He knows your sorrows and broken heart. He knows your weaknesses and strengths. He has numbered the hairs on your head. He has collected your tears in a bottle, and He has written all of your prayers in a book. He has collected all of your good works to be tallied up for your reward. He extends His hand and feeds all of His creation from His palm. There is nothing that is going on in your life that He doesn't know about.

He sees it all and knows it all. And He still loves you. You are not a mystery to God. You are His beautiful work of art, his daughter, and His plans for you are good. He has plans to prosper you and give you the desires of your heart—godly desires—for what is true, honest, just, pure, right, lovely and virtuous. (See Philippians 4:8)

Because God created the universe and everything in it, all things consist of Him—including you. As the psalmist said in Psalm 139:14: "I am fearfully and wonderfully made." That means you are worth the best God has for you. But you can't know what that best is if you are struggling secretly with pornography, jealousy, thievery, infidelity, relationship addictions, leading a double life, and all the other behaviors that hold you back.

So come out of hiding and become transparent before God and man. Take that first step towards wholeness. You won't be sorry.

APPENDIX

THE UNSUPERVISED WOMAN

Appendix

A word for early-maturing teen girls and their moms

What is early maturing?

Are you an early-maturing girl? In plain words, this girl can be defined as one who has experienced a more rapid growth into puberty than the average.

In the 1840s, American girls experienced their first menstruations on average at the age of seventeen. Today the average age of menarche is twelve. Statistically, the average age of menarche seems to be declining at an average age of about four months per decade for the past 100 years (Petersen 1979).

Imagine a three-year-old girl with fully developed breasts or a small boy with the deep voice of a man. Studies are estimating that by the year 2250, puberty would arrive that soon if physical development keeps up the current pace. (Santrock 1996). We are seeing this continuing change due to high levels of nutrition and conscientious health practices, increased standards of living, and of course advances in the sciences, especially in North America.

Females usually experience hormonal and body changes earlier than their male counterparts do. Girls will experiences height spurts, menarche, breast growth, pubic hair, and wider weight distribution.

I find it amazing how God has constructed the female anatomy. Her body can attract a sperm to her egg, conceive a child, grow a child within her body, feed the child there for nine months, birth a fully developed baby through her birth canal, and then continue to feed the child from her body. Amazing! And in many cases, a female at the ripe age of twelve years can accomplish all of the above in her early-matured body. Ladies, you are totally amazing!

What steps can I take to avoid the vulnerabilities of an early-maturing girl?

1. First, realize that you are a beautiful blessing of God. You are amazing, and God has wondrous plans for you to prosper and to succeed. Your early womanly beauty is not a curse or deficit. Be thankful for your attractiveness, for it's a gift from God. With proper training and education, coupled with your physical attributes, you will be a force to be reckoned with, to be sure!

2. Next, it's important for you dress in an age-appropriate way that also ensures modesty. If you use make up or wear jewelry, do so tastefully. Don't misunderstand me; it is certain-

ly not expected of you to dress like a Quaker, an Amish, or Mennonite girl, covered from neck to ankle.

3. Be conscious of older boys and even older men who are attracted to you. Remember, you are a minor, and it's inappropriate and certainly illegal for males over eighteen to approach you with romantic or physical interests. You must be truthful with these boys, explaining plainly how old you are and that you are not interested in establishing any type of friendship that requires you to be alone with them for any reason.

4. Be aware that relationships with older boys and young men will ostracize you from your family and peer group friends. You may have to live in secret rendezvous with him because being together is not sociably acceptable. Any relationship that requires you to live unsupervised or in secret cannot be right. You may believe that "No one understands me;" or "He's different than the rest;" or "We have a plan to get married and we are not breaking up;" or even, "We plan to run away together." These statements and others are sure signs of a relationship that will damage or destroy your relationships with your mom and dad, your siblings, and friends. It will also impact your future educationally, financially, and spiritually.

5. Recognize your mood swings. Your intuition, your spiritual discernment, and yes, even your logic is trying to tell you that this relationship is wrong. If you find yourself having strange or erratic moods, depression, emotional explosions,

loneliness and confusion–then listen to yourself and return to your age-appropriate life with your friends, family, and school environment. Remember there is something wrong with a much older boy who seems to be attracted to a girl who is way too young for him. Why isn't he dating girls his own age? Why isn't he respectful to your youth, your parents and your friend's wishes to keep you in an age-appropriate environment?

6. Stay in school! Graduate high school and aspire to higher education. Too many early-maturing girls seem to focus on their wedding day, obsess with getting married, and ignore their own self-improvements because of fear of not being married. Your wedding day will come soon enough, and in the meantime, become attractive by getting a higher education, amazing academic or technical skills. Become a valuable Proverbs 31 woman who participates in the betterment of your future family. Do you want to marry a future lawyer? Go to law school. Do you want to marry a future doctor? Go to nursing or medical school. Do you want to marry a future successful businessman? Go to college.

7. Stay in church! Attend as many church services as possible. This will expose you to great and useful Christian values, not to mention Christian boys who have a heart for God. Remember to not unequally yoke yourself with ungodly or unchristian males. Do not assume that you will be able to "save" your future husband once you have married him. If he doesn't comprehend your love for God, he is not of like-mind

and probably not a Christian. Marrying outside of the faith is a recipe for years of sorrow and anguish, especially when you have children who will not want to follow your Christian heritage, but will prefer to follow your husband's unbelieving lifestyle. Marry a Christian man when you get old enough to marry.

So, an early-maturing body can certainly come with mixed emotions. You can so enjoy the gift of attractiveness that God has blessed you with in such a young age. But it comes with great challenges of not relying upon your physical endowment or your gregarious presence. The responsibilities you are presented to yourself is to give you the best future as possible, which would include a good education, a close walk with God, and a consciousness that you are to enjoy your childhood and youth with those your own age – you owe this to yourself!

REFERENCES

Reference List

Antonucci, T.C. 1990. Social Supports and Social Relationships. New York: Academy Press.

Brooks-Gunn, J., Warren, M.P. April 1989. "How important are pubertal and social events for different problem behaviors and contexts?" Paper presented at the biennial meeting of the Society for Research in Child Development, Kansas City.

Butler, R.N. 1963. "The Life Review" Psychiatry.

Cassell, C. 1984. Swept Away: Why women fear their own sexuality. New York: Simon & Schuster.

Coleman, J. 1988. Intimate Relationships, Marriage and Family. New York: Macmillan.

Davis, K.E. 1985. "Near and Dear: Friendship and Love Compared." Psychology Today.

Helgeson, V.S. 1994. "Relationship to agency and communion to well being." Psychology Bulletin.

Hoyer, W.J., Rybash, J.M., Roodin, P.A. 1991. Adult Development and Aging, 4th Ed.,McGraw-Hill.

Kiecolt-Glasser, J.K., Malarkey, W.B., Chee, M., Newton, T., Cacioppo, J.T., Mao, H., Glaser, R. 1993. "Negative behavior during marital conflict." Psychosomatic Medicine

Lowenthal, M., Thurnher, M., Chiriboga, D. 1975. Four Stages of Life. San Francisco: Jossey-Bass.

Magnusson, D., Stattin, H., Allen, V.L.1985. "Biological Maturation and Social Development." Journal of Youth and Development.

Petersen, A.C. 1979. "Can puberty come faster?" Psychology Today, January.

Rybash, J.M., Roodin, P.A., & Santrock, J.W. 1991. Adult Development and Aging (2nd Ed.) Dubuque, IA: C. Brown.

Santrock, J.W. 1996. Child Development (7th Ed.). Brown and Benchmark Publishers.

Sarason, I.G., Sarason, B.R., Pierce, G.R. 1989. Social Support: An interactional view. NY: Wiley.

Stattin, H., Magnusson, D. 1990. Pubertal Maturation in female development (Vol. 2.). Hillsdale, NJ: Erlbaum.

CPSIA information can be obtained at www.ICGtesting.com
Printed in the USA
LVOW100744050613

337051LV00002B/6/P